You're Hired!

How to Get Your Dream Job *Online*

By

Chris Divivo

For more information, visit us at https://divivo.com

Or contact us at youre-hired@divivo.com

First Edition: March 2023

ISBN - Paperback: 979-8-39317-903-8

ISBN - eBook: 979-8-89034-062-7

DEDICATION

This book is dedicated to all people who don't want to get up on Monday morning… I hope this book will help you find a good reason to do so!

INTRODUCTION

'Everyone has been made for some particular work, and the desire for that work has been put in every heart.' - Rumi

Most materials that help you find a job focus on resumes or interviews. By all means, those are two essential steps in getting a job, and this book has plenty of materials to address those. However, we also emphasize your inner self, passion, talents, and competencies. Not only will we help you find a job, but we will also make sure it is a job you love, a dream job!

Some people's dream job might be to sit on a white sand beach and sip cocktails. Although spending our life on "vacation" sound very attractive, it might not be as fulfilling as a purposeful life. If that is your dream job, it might simply be because you never really had a professional activity that you profoundly enjoyed. Keep reading this book; it is designed to help you find exactly that, a job for which you wake up in the morning before the alarm even rings, a job that keeps you at night because you are full of ideas.

We all have the desire to contribute to the community to one extent, or another is rooted in our human nature. As social beings, we thrive in communities where we can connect, share, and support one another. The desire to contribute to the community is born out of our innate sense of empathy, compassion, and the need to be a part of something greater than ourselves. We feel a sense of purpose, fulfillment, and connectedness when we contribute. We become a part of a collective effort to make the world a better place, and that sense of belonging can be incredibly empowering and motivating.

The desire to contribute is coded in our genes; the problem is that if we spend too much time doing something we don't like, then that innate feeling dies deep inside our souls. And our dream job becomes a distant thought until the day it is forgotten. The aim of this book is not only to revive that dream but also to help you through the steps of achieving it.

A dream job is a job that is fulfilling and satisfying to you. It is a job that aligns with your strengths, interests, and passions and allows you to use your skills and abilities to your full potential. A dream job provides a sense of purpose and meaning and allows for personal and professional growth. It is also a job that provides a desirable work environment and culture and offers opportunities for advancement and success. Ultimately, a dream job makes an individual happy and fulfilled in their work—one which makes you jump out of bed every morning.

Dream Job! Is It Just A Dream?

"The biggest mistake people make in life is not trying to make a living at doing what they most enjoy." - Malcolm Forbes

Finding your dream job can be challenging when you have no idea where to start. This book intends to guide you through identifying your dream job and securing a position in a company you would love to work for. Here is an overview of the steps to find your dream job:

- Find your calling: Reflect on your strengths and interests before looking for a job. You can't find your dream job if you don't even know what your dreams are. This chapter will help you identify the type of position that will be fulfilling and satisfying for you. Please don't overlook this step; it is the foundation of enjoyable work.

- Identify your industry: once you have a general idea of the work you are looking for, start researching different industries and companies that align with your interests, competencies, and lifestyle. This will give you a better idea of the available job opportunities and which companies may be a good fit for you. The better your knowledge about your industry, the higher the chance you are aiming for the correct position.

- Locate your hunting ground: Nowadays, there are a lot of online resources it could be overwhelming to know where even to start. We did the groundwork for you and outlined great resources. Networking in the right community is another essential part of the job search process. Attend industry events, join professional organizations, and reach out to your connections to learn more about job opportunities and make new connections.

- Submit irresistible applications: ensure your resume and cover letter are up-to-date and tailored to the job you are applying for. This will help you stand out from other applicants and showcase your skills and qualifications. Focus on your achievement and competency, and remember that securing a job is a sales job; you are selling your personal brand.

- Ace your interviews: once you have identified potential job opportunities, start applying for jobs and prepare for interviews. Research the company and the job before the interview. Practice answering common interview questions to increase your confidence and chances of winning interviews.

Remember, stay persistent, continually networking and applying for jobs even if you don't get an immediate response. With dedication and focus, you will find a job you are passionate about and enjoy.

Online Job! Is That Possible?

"The purpose of life is to discover your gift. The meaning of life is to give your gift away." - David Viscott

An online job is a type of employment that allows an individual to work remotely using a computer and internet connection. Online work has become increasingly popular due to advancements in technology and communication tools and a growing desire among employees for work-life balance. Online jobs can take many forms, including telecommuting, freelance work, and virtual assisting. Many online jobs can be done from anywhere worldwide as long as the individual has a reliable internet connection.

One of the main advantages of online jobs is the flexibility they offer. With an online position, an individual can work from anywhere, anytime. This can especially appeal to those who need to work around other commitments, such as caring for children or elderly family members. Young adults might want to travel around the world but still need a job to sustain themselves, and an increasing number of cities offer co-working spaces to cater to working travelers. Another reason to work online is that you might be living in the countryside, and either there are no local jobs matching your skills, or they don't pay what you expect; working online is an excellent solution to address both issues. Online jobs also allow individuals to set their schedules, giving them the freedom to work when it is most convenient for them.

Another advantage of online jobs is the wide range of opportunities available. Online jobs are available in many industries, including marketing, customer service, writing, editing, and more. This means that individuals with diverse skills and interests can find an online job that aligns with their strengths and passions. In addition, online jobs can offer a more affordable and convenient alternative to traditional employment. Many online jobs do not require any upfront investment, such as purchasing specialized equipment or software. This makes it easier for individuals to start working immediately without incurring additional expenses.

Overall, online jobs offer several benefits, including flexibility, a wide range of opportunities, and affordability. With the increasing use of technology, the demand for online jobs is rapidly growing, providing individuals with more opportunities to work remotely and achieve a work-life balance.

Before we go any further, though, let's review some myths about online jobs that may discourage people from pursuing this type of work. One of the most common myths is that online jobs don't pay well. While very simple online jobs don't pay well, the online job scene has changed dramatically in the last few years, with many high-paying opportunities available. Not only will you find equivalent salaries, but in many instances, you might even get paid more for the same task because you have access to a worldwide market, giving you opportunities you might not have locally. Some people also believe that online jobs are easy, but most require a certain level of skill and effort. While some online jobs may be easier than others, you still need to be dedicated and hardworking to succeed. Another myth is that online jobs are only for tech-savvy people. While some online jobs, such as web development, require technical skills, many do not. For example, you can work as a virtual assistant, freelance writer, or teacher without advanced technical skills. Finally, some people believe that online jobs are not secure. While there is always some risk involved in any position, online jobs can be just as secure as traditional office jobs. Protecting your personal information and ensuring that you work with reputable companies and people is essential.

Ready to look for your first online job? Here are some things to consider when deciding if online work is suitable for you:

- Your ability to work independently: an online job requires high self-motivation and the ability to work independently without supervision. If you thrive in a structured work environment and need regular guidance and support from your manager, online work may not be a good fit for you.

- Your home environment: when working online, you need to have a dedicated workspace at home that is free from distractions and allows you to focus on your work. Creating an effective work environment at home may be challenging if you have a busy household with young children or pets or live in a noisy or crowded environment.

- Your work schedule: telecommuting typically requires a flexible work schedule, as you may need to be available outside of regular business hours to attend meetings or collaborate with colleagues in different time zones. If you have commitments that require fixed scheduling, it may be challenging to balance your work and personal life when telecommuting.

- Your personal preferences: ultimately, the decision to work online should be based on your personal preferences and what will make you happy and productive in your work. If you enjoy the social interaction and camaraderie of a traditional office setting, telecommuting may not be the right choice. But if you value flexibility, autonomy, and the ability to work from anywhere, telecommuting may be a great option.

Online jobs aren't all the same. So let's discuss how to assess online opportunities to determine which ones might be the perfect fit for you and if an online job is for you.

- Consider how much stability you seek: many ways to work remotely exist. You can work as a full-time employee for one company. You can work on a project basis for a few months at a time. You can also freelance for a variety of different companies. It's important to consider what kind of online opportunity will work for you. A full-time position might be your best bet if you seek stability and growth opportunities. But a contract or freelance position might be a better bet if you're looking for flexibility and freedom to work whenever and wherever you want.

- Think about when you want to work: with in-person jobs, your hours are pretty straightforward; you're expected to be at the office from 8 AM to 5 PM or whatever hours are standard for the company. But with online jobs, your work hours depend on several factors; company location, customer location, or flexibility. For example, if you are in Paris and teaching French to children in China, you have to be available at 3 AM to catch the morning session in China. Of course, you can look for companies that keep pretty traditional work hours in your time zone if that works best for you.

- Can you get benefits as an online worker? The answer is a yes, possible! You can have the same pay, benefits, and even better perks than working in an office. You have to know where to look. However, 80% of the time, No. You control your hours, clients, projects, and work environment as a freelancer. But you're also responsible for paying employment taxes and providing your health insurance, vacation time, and other benefits.

- Consider income security: as a freelancer, you may be paid for completing a project rather than an hourly rate, so income does not always come in on a reliable schedule. There's much freedom in freelancing but also a lot of added responsibility.

- Opportunity widely depends on the industry: Some industries easily accommodate online jobs, and others don't. For instance, if you are a manufacturing plant manager, it is impossible to fulfill that position without being present at the plant. However, that doesn't mean you can't find great online opportunities in the manufacturing industry.

Before you get entrenched in landing an online job, you must define what you value in life. Do you value freedom or security? Do you see yourself spending 10 hours daily in an office that drains your energy or being your own boss? Your answer will define if the online job is right for you!

Pros Of Online Work

- Flexibility: One of the most significant advantages of online work is choosing your schedule and working from anywhere with an internet connection. This can be especially beneficial for those who need a more flexible work arrangement due to family or personal commitments.

- Cost savings: Working online can also save you money on commuting costs, office attire, lunches, and other expenses associated with a traditional job.

- Increased productivity: Some people find they are more productive when working from home, as they can eliminate distractions and create a more focused work environment.

- Greater work-life balance: Online work can allow you to balance your professional and personal life better, as you have more control over your schedule.

- Access to a broader range of job opportunities: Working online can open up a whole world of job opportunities, as you are not limited to job openings in your local area.

Cons Of Online Work

- Lack of face-to-face interaction: One of the downsides of online work is the lack of face-to-face interaction with colleagues and clients. This can make building relationships more difficult and might lead to feelings of isolation.

- Technical issues: Working online can also bring a range of technical issues, such as problems with internet connectivity or computer malfunctions.

- Distractions at home: Focusing on work at home can be more challenging, as there may be more distractions and temptations.

- Limited benefits: Some online jobs may not offer the same benefits as traditional jobs, such as healthcare or retirement plans.

- Limited job security: The gig economy and short-term contracts are becoming more common in the online work world, which can lead to a lack of job security.

Are you decided? Yes, no? Read on, and let's dive into finding your dream job; then, you can determine if you want it to be online or onsite. Either way, you will find a wealth of resources in the following chapters to zero in on your dream job.

FIND YOUR CALLING

"The two most important days in your life are the day you are born, and the day you find out why." - Mark Twain

There is a reason why we start by figuring out what your calling is rather than working on your resume. For once, your resume is a history of your past, not necessarily an actual image of your current desires. Too often, people do studies based on parents' desires, friends' recommendations, or previous academic results. None of those accurately reflect who you are or even what you are capable of doing. When it comes to work experience, it follows a similar pattern; people find it so tedious and difficult to secure a job that they will take the first job offer and do their best to keep it. Few seek a better or different job while they are employed. Even fewer dare to change career paths to focus on something they love doing, even though it might mean starting from a lower position.

To secure your dream job, you first need to know your dream! In this chapter, we will help you figure out who you are, dig deeper into your aspirations, to find your calling. We will focus on five aspects:

- Your personality: personality refers to an individual's unique characteristics and traits that influence their behavior, thoughts, and emotions. Personality is often considered stable over time and shaped by genetics and growing up.

- Your passions: passion refers to a strong interest or enthusiasm for something. It is an emotional feeling that drives an individual to pursue a particular activity or subject with energy and dedication. Passion is often associated with a desire to make a difference or contribute to something larger than oneself.

- Your talents: talents refer to natural aptitudes or abilities that allow an individual to perform a particular activity or task easily and successfully. Talent is often considered a genetic/intrinsic trait but must also be developed through practice and experience.

- Your competencies: refer to the knowledge, skills, and abilities that enable an individual to perform a job effectively. They are often used as the basis for evaluating and developing employees' performance and may include problem-solving, communication, teamwork, and leadership. Competencies are usually acquired through education and training and can be improved through practice and experience.

Your personality is a set of characteristics and traits that influence your behavior, thoughts, and emotions. Your passion is an emotional feeling that drives you to pursue a particular activity or subject with energy and dedication. At the same time, your talent is a natural aptitude or ability for something that allows you to perform a particular activity or task with ease and success. Your competencies refer to skills you have acquired and can use in a specific context to deliver outstanding work.

IDENTIFY YOUR PERSONALITY

"Your personality is your unique blueprint that encompasses all the things that make you who you are." - Unknown

Knowing your personality can be highly beneficial in so many ways! It helps you understand your strengths, weaknesses, values, and motivations. This self-awareness can boost confidence and make communicating and getting along with others easier. It can also lead to success in both your personal and professional life.

One of the best things about understanding your personality is that it helps you be more self-aware. When you know what you're good at and not so good at, it's easier to focus on the things that come naturally to you. This can give you a big boost of confidence and make you feel more comfortable in your skin. Having a good understanding of your personality can also make communicating and getting along with others easier. When you know what makes you tick, it's easier to understand where other people are coming from too. This can lead to more robust and more positive relationships, whether it's with friends, family, colleagues, or clients. Finally, understanding your personality can help you achieve success in any area of your life. When you use your strengths and abilities correctly, you're more likely to excel and be successful. This can increase job satisfaction, career advancement, and fulfillment of personal relationships.

Some people believe personality tests are unproductive because they may not accurately reflect an individual's personality or behavior. They argue that these tests are often based on self-reported data, which can be biased or inaccurate. Additionally, some critics say that the test-taker can easily manipulate these tests, especially if they know what the test is measuring. Ignore the critic and give it a try. Taking those tests only requires a little time, and you will learn a few things about yourself, at least highlighting some traits. The best investment will always be in yourself; the better you know yourself, the better off you will be.

In short, knowing your personality is a big deal! It can give you confidence, help you communicate and get along with others, and lead to success in life. Take time to learn about yourself and what defines your unique personality – it'll be worth it!

Exercise 1: Formal Personality Type

"How many introverts does it take to change a light bulb? None, they prefer to stay in the dark."

There are many different theories and approaches to classifying personality types. Some of the most well-known and widely used systems include:

- The Five-Factor Model (FFM) is a system for classifying personality traits based on five key dimensions: openness, conscientiousness, extraversion, agreeableness, and neuroticism. These dimensions are considered stable over time and are believed to be important in predicting an individual's behavior and psychological well-being.

  https://psychology-tools.com/test/big-5-personality-test

- The Myers-Briggs Type Indicator (MBTI) categorizes individuals into 16 personality types based on their preferences for Introversion vs. Extraversion, Sensing vs. Intuition, Thinking vs. Feeling, and Judging vs. Perceiving. There are 16 personality types: ISTJ, ISFJ, INFJ, INTJ, ISTP, ISFP, INFP, INTP, ESTJ, ESFJ, ENFJ, ENTJ, ESTP, ESFP, ENFP, and ENTP.

  https://www.truity.com/test/type-finder-personality-test-new

- The Enneagram categorizes individuals into nine personality types based on their core motivations, fears, and values. The nine personality types are The Perfectionist, The Helper, The Achiever, The Individualist, The Investigator, The Loyalist, The Enthusiast, The Challenger, and The Peacemaker.

  https://www.psychologyjunkie.com/free-enneagram-test/

- The Holland Codes is a system for classifying personality types based on six interests: realistic, investigative, artistic, social, enterprising, and conventional. These interests are relatively stable over time and are believed to be related to an individual's career choices and preferences.

  https://www.truity.com/test/holland-code-career-test

It's important to note that these are just a few examples of the many different approaches to classifying personality types and that no single system is universally accepted or regarded as definitive.

To take a personality test, you must typically answer questions about your thoughts, feelings, and behaviors. The test will then use your responses to determine your personality type, which can be represented by a combination of letters, numbers, or other symbols. It is essential to remember that personality tests are not definitive measures of an individual's personality, and the results should be interpreted cautiously. However, they can provide valuable insights and be a helpful tool for self-discovery, but they should not be used to decide an individual's abilities or potential. Feel free to use the provided links to take some of those free personality tests and see what you come up with!

Exercise 2: Character Traits

"How many optimists does it take to change a light bulb? None, they just see the bright side of the situation."

If you are not into formal personality type tests, you can identify your character traits; they also reflect your personality. Let's have some fun. Go through the list and circle any quality or character that describes you. The goal is not to circle as many as you can. Instead, we recommend only circling the one you feel strongly about, as it will make it easier to narrow down your personality type. Ideally, you will pick a maximum of ten of them. Have fun! There are no right or wrong answers.

accomplished	charming	direct	funny
active	cheerful	discerning	gallant
adorable	chivalrous	distinguished	gentle
adventurous	communicative	down-to-earth	genuine
affectionate	compassionate	earnest	gifted
affluent	complex	earthy	glamorous
agreeable	confident	easygoing	good-natured
ambitious	confused	eccentric	graceful
amiable	conscientious	educated	gracious
amusing	conservative	elegant	greedy
angelic	considerate	delightful	happy
animated	cordial	empathetic	homebody
appealing	cosmopolitan	enchanting	honest
aristocratic	courteous	energetic	humanitarian
articulate	crazy	enterprising	humorous
artistic	creative	ethical	idealistic
assertive	cultured	even-tempered	idiosyncratic
assured	curious	exquisite	impish
athletic	cute	extraordinary	impulsive
attentive	cynical	extroverted	independent
audacious	daring	exuberant	individualistic
balanced	dashing	faithful	intelligent
bilingual	deliberate	fascinating	intense
bold	delicate	fearless	introspective
bright	dependable	fiery	intuitive
candid	desperate	finicky	inventive
captivating	devilish	flaky	jovial
caring	devoted	flexible	kind
cerebral	diligent	frank	kooky

laid back

liberal

lighthearted

literate

lively

lovely

loyal

mature

maverick

mellow

merry

mischievous

modest

natural

naturalist

nonconformist

observant

old-fashioned

opinionated

optimistic

original

outgoing

outrageous

outspoken

particular

patient

pauper

perceptive

personable

plastic

playful

poised

polished

polite

positive

practical

prosperous

quiet

rebellious

refined

reserved

responsible

reticent

robust

rocker

rogue

romantic

rugged

safe

seasoned

secure

self-assured

sensible

sensitive

sensuous

serene

shapely

sharp

sober

sociable

sophisticated

spirited

spiritual

spontaneous

sporty

stable

steady

strong

stylish

sunny

superficial

supportive

sweet

tactful

talented

talkative

tender

thoughtful

timid

tolerant

tomboy

traditional

tranquil

trustworthy

unconventional

understanding

unique

upbeat

urbane

vibrant

vigorous

vivacious

vulnerable

whimsical

wholesome

wild

wise

witty

wonderful

zealot

Once you have finished circling all your traits, you want to write them all in one list, from the most relevant to the least appropriate. It will give you a good idea of your most vital personality traits, refining your understanding of yourself.

Fun exercise, ask your spouse, partner, kids, or best friends to go through the list and circle what they think defines your personality traits. It will give you a perspective on how people perceive you, and you might be surprised how it compares to your own list.

	My List	Partner	Friend
Trait #1			
Trait #2			
Trait #3			
Trait #4			
Trait #5			
Trait #6			
Trait #7			
Trait #8			
Trait #9			
Trait #10			

Exercise 3: The Behavioral Matrix

"Why did the sailor behave so well during the storm? They didn't want to rock the boat!"

The behavioral matrix is a straightforward way to analyze your personality type. Use the following table to define if you are more "Formal" or "Informal" and if you are more "Dominant" or "Go With the Flow" person. Don't try to guess which one it would be best to be; there is no best answer, be honest with yourself and pick the most appropriate choice. It is about finding out who you are. Nobody is getting a grade. Put one X in each raw to define your level of formality and dominance. Do not pick the zero value.

	5	4	3	2	1	0	1	2	3	4	5	
Formal												Informal
Dominant												Go with Flow

Based on your X, below are your behavioral type:

- Formal and Dominant are called: **<u>Driver</u>**
- Formal and Go With the Flow are called: **<u>Analytical</u>**
- Informal and Dominant are called: **<u>Expressive</u>**
- Informal and Go With the Flow are called: **<u>Amiable</u>**

Once you define your type, read below the characteristic of your dominant style.

Driver: The Doer, the Optimist, and the Extrovert

Drivers are task-oriented and assertive. "My way or the highway" is the credo of the fast-paced, action-oriented Driver. Drivers are challenging people to convince because they believe they're always right. Drivers are bottom-line thinkers. They cut to the chase. Tell them when, where, how, why, and how much it will cost. If you become defensive and emotional, the Driver will lose respect for you. They are great debaters and love to win. Drivers are practical according to the bottom line. The driver is primarily left-brained.

Personality Factors:

Goal Oriented

Impatient

Task-Oriented

Workaholic

Demanding

Decisive

Time Effective

Blunt and bossy

Administrative

Opinionated

Innovative

Tends to use people

Dominates others

Decides for others

As a Friend:

Has little need for friends

Will work for group activity

Will lead and organize

Is usually right

Excels in emergencies

Knows everything

Can do everything better

Is too independent

Possessive of friends and mate

Can't say, "I'm sorry."

May be correct, but unpopular

Not easily discouraged

Enjoys controversy and arguments

Comes on too strong

Inflexible

Dislikes tears and emotions

Analytical: The Introvert, the Thinker, and the Pessimist

Analytical people are task-oriented and non-assertive. Every situation is thought out in advance. Please don't mess with their well-organized plans! They are not very spontaneous people. They think through everything and tend not to answer questions immediately, but when they do, their answers are rational and non-emotional. They are not big talkers but excellent listeners. The Analytical will challenge you if they think you're being illogical or exaggerating. They like proof and facts. They are detail-oriented. Their car and house will always be clean and orderly. They don't think highly of you if yours isn't. Analytical are primarily left-brained.

Personality Factors:

Planner

Detail-oriented

Slow decisions

Technical

Must be right

Conservative

Organizer

Low pressure

Logical

Precise

Problem solver

Persistent

Deep and thoughtful

Serious and purposeful

Self-sacrificing

Conscientious

Idealistic

Appreciative of beauty

As a Friend:

Makes friends cautiously

Content to stay in the background

Avoids causing attention

Faithful and devoted

Will listen to complaints

Can solve other's problems

Deep concern for other people

Moved to tears with compassion

Lives through others

Insecure socially

Withdrawn and remote

Critical of others

Holds back affection

Dislikes those in opposition

Suspicious of people

Antagonistic and vengeful

Unforgiving

Skeptical of compliments

Expressive: The Extrovert, the Talker, and the Optimist

Expressive people are people-oriented and assertive. These people are free-spirited, very outgoing, and spontaneous. Risk-taking is easy; experimenting with new foods, restaurants, and things to do will excite this personality. They are expressive with their feelings and are an emotional open book. The expressive is highly creative and constantly moving. Their ideas are better than anyone else's. Holding their attention is a challenge. They pride themselves on their spontaneity and impulsiveness. They might even offer hints on how you can improve. Expressive are primarily right-brained.

Personality Factors:

Fast decisions

Excitable

Enthusiastic

Compulsive talker

Exaggerates and elaborates

Dwells on trivial

Can't remember the names

Scares others off

Too happy for some

Has restless energy

Egotistical

Blusters and complains

Naive gets taken in

Has a loud voice and laugh

Controlled by circumstances

Gets angry easily

Seems phony to some

Never grows up

As a friend:

Makes friends easily

Loves people

Thrives on compliments

Seems exciting

Envied by others

Doesn't hold grudges

Apologizes quickly

Prevents dull moments

Likes spontaneous activities

Hates to be alone

Needs to be renter stage

Wants to be popular

Looks for credit

Dominates conversations

Interrupts and doesn't listen

Answers for others

Fickle and forgetful

Repeats stories

Amiable: The Introvert, the Watcher, and the Pessimist

Amiable people are people-oriented and non-assertive. These people like deep conversation and are sensitive and empathetic. They are friendly, polite, and supportive. They listen with a smile. They rarely ask questions or raise objections. They hate conflict and want to have a positive relationship with everyone. If you unintentionally offend them, they'll never tell you about it. Instead, they'll hide their hurt feelings until you leave, then vent their anger with their friends. These people are people pleasers, and hard to find out their truth, partly because they don't know and partly because they don't want to offend you. Amiable is primarily right-brained.

Personality Factors:

Needs people

Listener

Status quo

No risks

No pressure

Counselor

Questioning

Insecure

Supportive

No goals

No conflict

Soft hearted

Fearful and worried

Indecisive

Avoids responsibility

Too compromising

As a Friend:

Easy to get along with

Pleasant

Inoffensive

Good listener

Dry sense of humor

Enjoys watching people

Have many friends

Has compassion and concern

Dampens enthusiasm

Stays uninvolved

Is not exciting

Indifferent to plans

Judges others

Sarcastic and teasing

Resists change

IGNITE YOUR PASSIONS

"It's so hard when I have to, and so easy when I want to." - Sondra Anice Barnes

Do you love what you do for work? If not, it might be time to start thinking about the importance of having a passion for your job. Here's why.

First and foremost, when we are passionate about our jobs, we are happier at work. We look forward to working. And we find meaning and purpose in our daily tasks. This can lead to increased motivation and productivity since we are likelier to put in extra effort when we genuinely care about what we're doing. Also, having a passion for your job improves performance and success. When you're passionate about something, you're more likely to be engaged and put in the time and effort necessary to excel. Plus, you're more open to learning and growing since you're motivated by your love for the work and the desire to improve. All of this can lead to increased opportunities for advancement and success within the company.

Another great thing about having a passion for your job is that it can positively impact the work environment and culture. Employees who are passionate about their work tend to be more positive and energetic, making the office more enjoyable and productive. Plus, passionate employees are often more likely to inspire and motivate their coworkers, creating a more collaborative and supportive atmosphere. On top of all that, having a passion for your job can also help you achieve a better work-life balance. Finding a balance between our work and personal lives is easier when we love what we do. We're more likely to feel fulfilled and satisfied with our work, so we don't have to seek fulfillment and happiness through addictive behavior or superficial distraction. This can lead to a better overall quality of life.

Finally, having a passion for your job can give you greater purpose and fulfillment in life. When we're passionate about something, it becomes an integral part of our identity and a source of pride and satisfaction. This can help us feel more satisfied and fulfilled since we can profoundly contribute to something we care about. As you can see, having a passion for your work is essential for many reasons. It can lead to increased happiness, improved performance, a positive work environment, better work-life balance, and a greater sense of purpose and fulfillment. That's why it's so important to find a job you're genuinely passionate about and cultivate that passion for achieving success and happiness in your career.

That said, some people might value their work even if they don't feel a strong passion for it. One reason is that they may enjoy learning and developing new skills. Even if they don't feel a deep love for the work, they may enjoy mastering new techniques and seeing the results of their hard work. Another reason someone might enjoy their work is the social aspect of it. Work can be an opportunity to build relationships with colleagues or clients. Even if someone doesn't feel passionate about the work, they may enjoy their interactions with others.

Additionally, someone may find meaning, fulfillment, and satisfaction from helping others or knowing that their work contributes to the greater good. For many people, the most crucial aspect of their work may be the financial stability it provides. They may not feel passionate about the work but appreciate their job's security and stability. It could also be that someone temporarily sacrifices enjoyment in the job because they see potential opportunities it provides for career advancement. They may be motivated by the prospect of gaining new responsibilities, earning promotions, or building a solid resume.

Some people argue that passion is overrated. Finding a niche with great potential is better. Focus on the necessary skills to become the best at it, and then learn to love your work. It seems similar to saying: "You should marry a man with great potential and then learn to love him." It sometimes works; it even has an expression: "gold digger." And despite the negative connotation in some cases, it works as long as both parties know why they are together and agree to the untold agreement.

Passion is not required, but it sure helps make the day pass with more joy. Goals and focus are also powerful motivators to get out of bed before the alarm clock, but how long does it last, and what are all the compromises you are making when your reason for being is sheer force and willpower? Passion leads to enjoyment; enjoyment brings presence, and presence brings peace and meaning. By all means, anyone who has lived long enough knows that passion can change over time. Indeed, some people have several passions, and others change them many times throughout their life. In fact, in many instances, one might call something a passion because they like it and find pleasure in that activity but don't know yet that they might have a more profound passion for something else. How would I know I have a passion for something I don't know exists or have not yet experienced? Finding a passion requires being willing to experience new activities and be curious about the world around us to maybe stubble on something we discover a deep passion for. Steve Jobs was not born passionate about designing computers, but it sure seems that he stubble upon his great passion. Follow your heart, and it will lead you to your passion.

One thing is clear though the system in which we currently live does its best to drive us away from anything we might be passionate about. Somehow after a few years of schooling, we all want to be a doctor, an engineer, or a lawyer. Why? Whoever can't make it or qualify for one of those professions takes the jobs left. Could it be that this is the reason why so many people are not satisfied with their professional activity? I don't remember a class that taught me how to figure out what I would love to do. Instead, I clearly remember the mantra work hard to get good grades because good grades will lend to a good job, and a good job will allow having many things and having things will make us happy. By all means, passion is not a fix it all solution. However, I would argue that for most people, reconnecting with something they love doing will undoubtedly bring some much-needed light and joy into their life.

How To Find My Passion?

"Don't ask yourself what the world needs; ask yourself what makes you come alive. And then go and do that. Because what the world needs is people who have come alive." - Harold Whitman

There is no one-size-fits-all answer on how to ignite your passion, as what inspires passion in one person may affect another differently. However, here are a few ideas that might help you to find your passion.

One of the first steps to finding your passion is to reflect on your interests. What activities do you enjoy doing in your free time? What topics or hobbies fascinate you? Start by listing everything you're interested in, no matter how small or insignificant it may seem. Sometimes, your passion can be right before you; it just takes a little self-reflection to recognize it.

It's easy to get stuck in a rut, doing the same things daily. Trying new things can be a great way to spark your passion and open yourself up to new opportunities. Take a class in something you've always been interested in, attend gatherings and network with new people. When you come across something that fascinates you, pursue it! Whether it's a new hobby, a subject you'd like to learn more about, or a problem you want to solve, following your curiosity can lead you to new and exciting things.

Pay attention to what makes you lose track of time. Have you ever been so absorbed in something that you lost track of time? Please pay attention to those moments, as they can be a clue to your passions. Whether it's a sport, something you are designing or crafting, a new subject you are learning about, or a cause you are working for, these activities can give you a sense of flow and fulfillment that can help guide you toward your passion.

Consider your natural talents. More often than not, our passions are linked to our natural talents. Think about the things that come quickly to you or the things that others often compliment you on. These talents can be a clue to your passions and help guide you toward a career or hobby that will bring you joy and fulfillment.

Reflect on your values and beliefs. What are the things that matter most to you? What causes or issues do you feel strongly about? Consider how you can align your passions with your values and positively impact the world. Your passions may be linked to your values and beliefs and involve making a difference in the world.

Finding your passion can be a process of trial and error, so don't be afraid to make mistakes along the way. Every experience can teach you something new about yourself and what you're genuinely passionate about. Seek inspiration from books, documentaries, or events related to your interests. Surround yourself with people who inspire you and support your goals. Staying motivated and focused on finding your passion is easier when feeling inspired.

Once you've identified your passions, learning and growing in those areas is essential. Look for opportunities to take classes or workshops, read books or articles, or find a mentor who can help guide you in your journey. The more you know about your passion, the easier it will be to find ways to incorporate it into your career.

Surrounding yourself with positive people who support and encourage you can significantly impact your mindset and motivation. Seek out colleagues or friends who share your passions, and join clubs or groups related to your interests. Being part of a community can help you deepen your understanding of your passion and provide opportunities for collaboration and growth.

It's hard to be passionate about anything without caring for yourself. When you're feeling healthy and balanced, it's easier to be aligned with yourself and listen to your inner guidance, which constantly tries to lead you toward your passions. Ensure you get enough sleep, eat well, and take time for self-care activities like exercise or meditation.

Let's also remember that passions can change over time, and that's perfectly okay. As we grow and evolve, our interests and priorities can shift, and what we were once passionate about may no longer hold the same appeal. We must permit ourselves to explore new passions and interests and let go of the things that no longer bring us the same fulfillment. Embracing change and being open to new experiences can lead us down exciting new paths and help us discover new passions that we never even knew existed. So if you find that your desires are changing, embrace the journey and see where it takes you – you never know what unique new experiences, opportunities, and jobs may be waiting just around the corner.

In conclusion, igniting your passion requires effort and self-reflection, but the rewards can be enormous. By identifying and exploring your interests, seeking new opportunities to learn and grow, paying attention to what makes you lose track of time, and seeking inspiration, you can uncover your passion and find greater happiness and fulfillment in your life and career. So go out there and start exploring – the world awaits you!

Exercise

"Why did the passionate artist quit his day job? He wanted to pursue his true passion – drawing outside the lines!"

In this section, you will find some exercises aimed at helping you identify your passions. In this first part, you will look at past or present activities you feel passionate about. This exercise is free-flowing and very open. Just go through the questions and jot down your answers. If a question does not inspire you, go to the next one. However, make sure you answer at least three different questions. Life is too short to spend it doing something you don't like to do. Life isn't about doing more but rather about doing something you genuinely enjoy doing. Late in your life, when contemplating your life, what will matter is not how much you have but all those moments you enjoy being yourself.

- What do I love to do?
- What are my most incredible moments of happiness?
- What would I be doing right now if money were no object?
- What is my secret ambition?
- What activities do I most enjoy doing?
- What motivates me in life?
- What were my favorite things to do as a child?
- What are my hobbies?

- What am I fascinated with?
- What would I do if I knew I could not fail?
- What activities make me lose track of time?
- What types of books or magazines do I purchase?

What about the things you don't like doing?

You may ask yourself, what this has to do with my passions? It has been said that nothing exists without its opposite. Hence, if you are still unclear about your passions, you likely know what you don't like to do. Make a quick list of things, activities, roles, or tasks that you don't want to do:

-
-
-

There is another reason you want to be more conscious about what you don't like doing. If you stop doing the things you don't like, you are well on your way to doing more of what you love to do – and finding ways to associate with other people to do what you don't want to do.

Let's Anchor It!

Well done! Go back to your answers and make a list of your passions. Classify them from the most to the least exciting ones. When choosing, listen to your heart, and don't let your fear or judgment get in the way. Also, for each passion, specify the reasons you feel so compelled. Why do you have such a strong desire regarding that passion? You want to identify the feeling for that passion rather than the activity. For instance, let's say one of your passion is travel. The reason could be that you like: meeting new people, discovering new places, learning about new cultures, trying different foods and dishes, etc… The passion might not come from the specific activity but from everything linked while doing that activity.

Once you have identified one or several of your passion, pounder on the following idea to anchor the idea of living your passion.

- What would be the benefits for you to live your passion?
- What are the consequences of not living your passions?
- What are the roadblocks in your way to living your passions?
- How could you overcome those obstacles?
- What is the first step I can take toward my passion?
- Start somewhere and keep walking...

UNCOVER YOUR TALENTS

"Use what talent you possess: the woods would be very silent if no birds sang except those that sang best." - Henry Van Dyke

Have you ever felt utterly unfulfilled in a job, like you were going through the motions and not making a difference? You didn't feel as if you were using your strengths or abilities to their full potential. On the other hand, have you ever taken on an endeavor where you felt like you were making a difference without any effort, where you felt like you were using your natural talents and abilities to the fullest? If so, you know firsthand the benefits of doing a job aligned with your abilities.

You are more likely to feel motivated, engaged, and fulfilled when you do a job that aligns with your talents. When you can use your strengths and abilities to their full potential, it can be incredibly satisfying and rewarding. You are more likely to feel like you are making a real contribution and adding value to your organization or team. Not only that but usually, the tasks seem effortless since you use natural gifts.

Moreover, the benefits of doing a job aligned with your talents go beyond just feeling good about your work. Studies have shown that people who can use their strengths and abilities at work are more likely to be successful and have higher levels of job satisfaction. They are also more likely to experience better physical and mental health and lower levels of stress and burnout. Finally, doing a job aligned with one's talents can lead to career advancement and success. When individuals can use their natural strengths and abilities in their work, they are more likely to excel and be recognized for their achievements. This can lead to promotions and other opportunities for advancement within the organization.

Some people believe that talents or personal gifts are overrated because they see them as secondary to hard work and dedication. They argue that putting too much emphasis on natural abilities can demotivate those who may not possess the same talents. Additionally, some may believe that relying solely on talents can lead to complacency and a lack of effort, whereas putting in the time and effort to develop a skill can lead to tremendous success in the long run. Furthermore, it is argued that the focus on talent overlooks the importance of other factors, such as experience, education, and networking, which can contribute to success in various fields. All those points might be well-meant, but in the end, we have all observed that, most often than not, people who standout out on a field usually have something more than just hard work; it almost seems they were born for that activity.

Some people believe they lack talent or special skills and therefore are discouraged when pursuing their goals and aspirations. However, it's important to remember that everyone has unique strengths and abilities, which may not always fit into traditional definitions of "talent." The problem is that we think only those like Tiger Hood, Michael Jackson, or Ludwig van Beethoven have talents. What about the middle-grade teacher who is so motivating and pedagogic that she gets her least-performing students and transforms them into avid learners? Everyone has talents. Unfortunately, many people have been led to believe that talents are reserved for special people. I have observed that anyone who thinks they don't have any talent usually has not looked closely enough or doesn't acknowledge some of their obvious talents. Keep reading, and let's find your talents together.

How To Uncover Your Talents?

Your talent is God's gift to you. What you do with it is your gift back to God.' - Leo Buscaglia

How would you find your talents if you don't know them yet? Uncovering your talents can seem daunting, especially if you believe you have none.

Everyone has talents, but some people find it challenging to identify them. If you feel like you don't have any talents, don't worry - it's common to underestimate your abilities. The first step to uncovering your talents is to explore your interests. What do you enjoy doing in your free time? What topics or activities do you find yourself constantly drawn to? You may uncover hidden talents by taking the time to reflect on your interests and past successes. Think about times in your life when you felt successful. What were you doing? What made you feel accomplished? How did you succeed? Did those accomplishments come with ease? These successes could be clues to your talents.

It's also helpful to seek feedback from others. Talk to your friends, family, and colleagues about your strengths and ask for their honest opinion. They can provide insights that you haven't considered. Do people tell you that you have a way with words? Are you great at planning parties? Please take note of these compliments because they could be indications of your talents.

Additionally, consider trying new things and stepping out of your comfort zone. Take a class, join a club or volunteer for an organization. By exposing yourself to new experiences, you may discover talents that you never knew you had. It's essential to remember that talents come in many forms and don't have to be traditional skills like playing an instrument or speaking multiple languages. Some talents include qualities like empathy, creativity, and problem-solving skills. By reframing your perspective on what constitutes talent, you can identify strengths you never realized you possessed.

Natural talents can be found in different areas of life. These areas include physical abilities such as physical strength, coordination, spatial awareness, bodily-kinesthetic skills, manual speed, and accuracy. Additionally, mental abilities include analytical reasoning, organization, management talents, logical, mathematical, associative memory, visual dexterity, abstract concept, and problem-solving. Social skills, such as empathy, personal interaction, networking, intrapersonal skills, and intuition, can also be crucial to one's natural talents. Finally, creative and artistic abilities such as art, linguistic skills, musical talent, creativity, and forethought could help uncover one's natural talents.

Be patient and kind to yourself throughout the process. Uncovering your talents is a journey, and it's essential to recognize that it may take time. Celebrate small wins and avoid getting discouraged if you have not discovered your talents. Remember, everyone has unique gifts to offer, and by uncovering yours, you will find greater fulfillment and purpose in your life.

Exercise

Every individual possesses unique talents and personal gifts. Striving in life is not only about perfecting skills but also about mining the natural talents that one already has. Doing more of what you do best is more fulfilling and enriches and benefits the world.

Here are a few questions you could ask yourself to help you uncover your talents:

- What activities do I find myself naturally drawn to?
- What am I good at?
- What have you learned easily and rapidly?
- What type of things comes easily to me?
- What do others see as my strengths, natural abilities, and talents?
- What are your spontaneous reactions in unexpected situations?
- What challenges or obstacles have I overcome, and how did I do it?
- What makes me happy and fulfilled?
- What could I teach?
- Reflect on situations or events you have been successful and which might have been unexpected. Remember, talents can be physical, mental, or social.

Asking yourself these questions can help you explore your strengths and provide valuable insights into your talents and potential. Another way to find your abilities is to recall when you overcame obstacles. Quite often, talents are revealed in challenging times. We face some issues, and our natural talents kick in to help us overcome those hurdles. It is also essential to be open-minded and willing to try new things, as this can help you discover talents and interests that you may not have known you had.

EVALUATE YOUR COMPETENCIES

Competencies are abilities you acquire throughout your life, intentionally or by exposure. Transferable skills are not specific to any particular job but can be applied to various roles. In recent years, the term "competency" has gained significant attention in human resources. You may encounter a competency-based or competency-focused interview, during which the interviewer will ask questions to determine your level of competency in the required areas rather than just confirming the information in your resume. Competencies are critical; most people focus only on their trade skills. However, how useful in team setup is a graphic designer who has poor communication skills and can't communicate or understand the requirements and needs of the team correctly? What about the outstanding developer who can't keep a deadline and always deliver with many delays? On the other hand, an individual with excellent competencies will be an indispensable asset to the organization even though their skills related to the trade itself might be average. Projects are always delivered by a team; the better the teammates work together, the better the results. We see that in team sports, it is not enough to have the best player on your team; you need everyone else to add value and bring cohesion to the team.

Competencies fall into broad categories, such as those described below. We ordered them from the most important relating to any job to competencies more relevant to management positions or individuals aspiring to a management position. Work on each competency, starting with the first; it will add tremendous value to your candidacy and improve your chance of zeroing in on your dream job.

Time Management

"The key is not to prioritize what's on your schedule, but to schedule your priorities." - Stephen Covey

Time management skill refers to the ability to use time effectively and efficiently. It involves planning and organizing tasks and activities, setting priorities, and allocating time to achieve specific goals and objectives. Effective time management allows individuals to complete tasks on time, reduce stress, and improve productivity. It also involves recognizing and eliminating time-wasting activities and prioritizing tasks according to their importance and urgency. Good time management skills can be developed through various techniques, such as creating schedules, setting goals, delegating tasks, and avoiding distractions.

Critical Thinking

"A wise man makes his own decisions, an ignorant man follows public opinion." - Chinese Proverb

Critical thinking is the abilities that are required to evaluate information, consider options, and make informed and effective choices. Critical thinking involves identifying and defining problems, gathering and analyzing data, considering multiple perspectives, and making well-reasoned and justifiable decisions. Practical problem-solving skills can help individuals and organizations make informed and effective choices and can be critical in various professional contexts, including business, finance, and healthcare. Training, experience, and self-reflection can develop and improve critical thinking.

Strategic Thinking

"Strategic thinking is not a skill to be learned, but a mindset to be developed. It is a way of looking at the world and understanding how to navigate through it to get where you want to go." - Unknown

Strategic thinking analyzes and evaluates information, situations, and opportunities to develop and implement effective plans and strategies. It involves looking at the bigger picture, considering a wide range of options and factors, and making thoughtful and informed decisions that can help to achieve the desired outcome. Strategic thinkers can identify and prioritize goals, develop plans to achieve them, and adapt and adjust their strategies in response to changing circumstances. Strategic thinking is a required skill in many professional fields, as it can help individuals and organizations to achieve their goals and to make the most of opportunities and challenges.

Drive For Achievement

The drive for achievement is a term that refers to a person's desire to succeed, accomplish goals, and achieve recognition and success. People with a strong drive for achievement are often highly motivated and focused on achieving success in their chosen field or pursuit. They are willing to put in the hard work and effort necessary to achieve their goals and are often willing to take risks and face challenges to succeed. They are generally positive and enthusiastic, do not suffer too greatly from setbacks, and are tenacious; they are resourceful and self-driven; they can accept change and are flexible. A strong drive for achievement can be a powerful motivator and help people reach their full potential and achieve their goals.

Relationship Building

Relationship building is the process of establishing and maintaining positive, productive, and effective relationships with others. It involves developing a rapport and a connection with others, building trust and credibility, and working together to achieve common goals. Relationship building is a necessary skill in many professional and personal contexts. It can help individuals and organizations build supportive networks and develop mutually beneficial partnerships and collaborations. Effective relationship building requires good communication skills, empathy, and an understanding of the needs and interests of others. It also involves being able to manage conflicts and challenges constructively and positively.

Teamwork

"Talent wins games, but teamwork and intelligence win championships." - Michael Jordan

Teamwork skills are the abilities and qualities that enable a person to work effectively as part of a team. These skills include communication, collaboration, problem-solving, adaptability, conflict resolution, leadership, and delegating tasks and responsibilities. Teamwork skills are essential in any setting where individuals must work together towards a common goal, such as in a workplace, school, or sports team. These skills help team members to coordinate their efforts, support each other, and achieve their objectives more efficiently and effectively.

Continuous Improvement

"Continuous improvement is better than delayed perfection." - Mark Twain

Continuous improvement is an essential concept in many industries, as it can help organizations to improve efficiency, productivity, quality, and customer satisfaction. Continuous improvement is continually identifying and implementing ways to improve processes, products, services, and systems. It involves a proactive and ongoing approach to identifying and addressing areas for improvement. It can involve a range of activities, such as analyzing data, gathering feedback, and experimenting with new ideas and methods. Continuous improvement requires a mindset of constant learning and improvement and can be facilitated using tools and techniques such as Lean, Six Sigma, and Total Quality Management.

Customer Service

"The customer's perception is your reality." - Kate Zabriskie

Customer service is the ability to understand and meet the needs and expectations of customers. It involves profoundly understanding customer behavior, preferences, and expectations and using that knowledge to develop products, services, and experiences that meet or exceed those expectations. Customer service is an imperative skill to master in many professional fields, particularly in customer-facing industries such as retail, hospitality, and healthcare. It requires a combination of empathy, communication skills, and an understanding of the needs and motivations of customers. Whatever your field, you always have customers, even if you only deliver your work to your boss. Effective customer service can help to build strong relationships, increase customer satisfaction and loyalty, and drive business success.

Influencing Skills

'To be persuasive, we must be believable; to be believable, we must be credible; to be credible, we must be truthful.' - Edward R. Murrow

Influencing skills are the abilities that are required to persuade and motivate others to support a particular idea, course of action, or decision. Influencing skills involve communicating effectively, building rapport and relationships, and using various tactics and strategies to persuade and motivate others. Influencing skills are essential in many professional contexts. They can help individuals and organizations achieve their goals and build support and buy-in for their ideas and proposals. Influencing skills can be developed through training, experience, and self-reflection.

Change Management

'Change is the only constant in life. Those who embrace it and can adapt to it are the ones who will thrive and succeed in the long run. It's not about avoiding change; it's about leading it and shaping it to your advantage.' - John C. Maxwell

Change management refers to the ability of a leader to guide and support an organization or team through a process of change. This can involve developing and implementing strategies and plans to achieve the desired outcome, managing and mitigating the risks and challenges associated with change, and engaging and motivating others to support and contribute to the change process. Change management requires strategic thinking, communication skills, and the ability to manage complex situations and relationships. It is a critical skill in many professional contexts, as organizations and teams often need to adapt and evolve in response to changing environments, markets, and technologies.

Business Acumen

"The true test of a business leader is the ability to anticipate and adapt to change. Those who can do so will thrive, while those who resist change will struggle." - Peter Drucker

Business acumen, or commercial awareness, is understanding and analyzing the economic, financial, and market forces that impact an organization or industry. It involves understanding the key drivers of success in a given market or sector and businesses' challenges and opportunities. Business acumen is an essential skill for professionals in many fields, including business, finance, marketing, and sales, as it can help them to make informed and effective decisions and to develop successful strategies. Business acumen requires a broad understanding of business and economic principles and an ability to think critically and analytically.

Personal Growth & Mentoring

"The only person you should try to be better than is the person you were yesterday." - Unknown

Developing self and others is a process of personal and professional growth that involves increasing one's knowledge, skills, and abilities and helping others do the same. This can include learning new things, setting and working towards goals, seeking new experiences and challenges, and providing support, guidance, and encouragement to others. The purpose of this type of development is to improve one's abilities and quality of life, as well as to support the growth and success of others.

Leadership

"A true leader has the confidence to stand alone, the courage to make tough decisions, and the compassion to listen to the needs of others. He does not set out to be a leader but becomes one by the equality of his actions and the integrity of his intent." - Douglas MacArthur

Leadership skills are the abilities and qualities to guide and manage others effectively. Leadership skills include various competencies, such as communication, problem-solving, decision-making, strategic thinking, conflict management, and motivation. Influential leaders use their leadership skills to inspire and guide their teams, set and achieve goals, and create a positive and productive work environment. Leadership skills are a must-have in many professional contexts and can be developed through training, experience, and self-reflection.

Invaluable Competencies

Competencies play a crucial role in the workplace as they outline the skills, knowledge, and behaviors required to perform a job effectively. These are the foundation of success in any profession, and employees who possess the necessary competencies are more likely to excel in their roles. Competencies provide a clear framework for measuring an employee's performance, identifying areas for improvement, and developing career paths. By establishing and nurturing competencies within the organization, employers can ensure that their workforce has the skills and abilities to meet business goals and stay competitive in the marketplace.

Human resource managers often clearly know the skills and competencies necessary for a particular job. During the interview, they will assess the candidate's level of competence in each of these areas. The ideal candidate will surpass the minimum requirements for each competence. However, it is rare to find someone who immediately meets all of the requirements for a job. In most cases, the candidate with the highest overall score will be offered the position.

It is important to remember that scoring lower on one or more competencies does not necessarily disqualify you from the job. An employer willing to invest in their employees' development may provide training to address any areas of weakness during the induction period. Therefore, it is crucial to communicate your willingness to learn and grow during the interview process.

When evaluating an individual's level of competence, employers often use a defined set of criteria to stratify their skills and abilities. These criteria can vary by organization but typically include a range of levels, from basic to advanced. For example, an employer may use the following levels to describe an individual's competence in a particular area:

- <u>Novice</u>: This level indicates that the individual has little or no experience in the area.

- <u>Basic</u>: This level indicates that the individual understands the concepts and can perform basic tasks related to the area.

- <u>Intermediate</u>: This level indicates that the individual understands the area well and can perform various related tasks.

- <u>Advanced</u>: This level indicates that the individual thoroughly understands the area and can perform complex related tasks.

- <u>Expert</u>: This level indicates that the individual has extensive knowledge and experience in the area and is considered an expert.

During an interview, the employer may ask the candidate to assess their level of competence in any of the relevant areas. The candidate's self-assessment and the employer's evaluation of their skills and experience will help determine the level of competence that the individual possesses in each area.

Working on your competencies is one of the easier ways to improve your employability. Competencies can be learned and improved at any time. Identifying your weak competency and improving on it can help you score better during an interview and will undoubtedly make a difference in your professional life.

Exercise

"Why did the competency-based hiring manager cross the road? To get to the other side of the skillset!"

Use the following table to define your level of competencies. You will notice some extra empty rows at the bottom for you to list the specific or technical competencies required in your chosen trade.

The first four competencies (time management, critical thinking, strategic thinking, and drive for achievement) are required by anyone. They are the foundation for all other competencies. The next four (relationship building, teamwork, continuous improvement, and customer service) are critical for anyone with ambition in their career and who aspires to move above entry-level jobs. The last competencies (influencing skills, change management, business acumen, mentoring, and leadership) are management-level competencies. Focus on those skills if you aspire to a manager position.

The next chapter will define the skills and competencies required for various professions. You can return to this table and determine which competencies you need to improve upon.

Competencies	Novice	Basic	Intermediate	Advanced	Expert
Time Management					
Critical Thinking					
Strategic Thinking					
Drive for Achievement					
Relationship Building					
Teamwork					
Continuous Improvement					
Customer Service					
Influencing Skills					
Change Management					
Business Acumen					
Mentoring					
Leadership					
Technical Skill #1					
Technical Skill #2					
Technical Skill #3					
Technical Skill #4					
Technical Skill #5					
Technical Skill #6					

CHOOSE A PROFESSION

'A skill set is nothing more than a commitment to a certain level of performance.' - Doug Pederson

Choosing a profession is a crucial decision as it significantly impacts our lives. It defines our future career path, income, and social status. The decision we make today can affect us for the rest of our lives, making it essential to consider our options carefully. Selecting the right profession requires thorough research, self-assessment, and a deep understanding of our interests, skills, and values.

In the previous chapters, we focus on getting to know yourself better, learning about personality type, finding your passions, uncovering your talents, and identifying your competencies. It is time to find a profession you will enjoy, a job aligned with your inner self. Research different professions and industries to better understand the job duties, requirements, and earning potential. It's also essential to think about your values and what is important to you in a career, such as work-life balance, job security, or opportunities for advancement. Additionally, networking with professionals in fields of interest can provide valuable insight into different professions' day-to-day work, challenges, and rewards. Remember that choosing a profession is not a one-time decision and may require ongoing exploration and adaptation. Moreover, with the proliferation of information and training materials, it is more accessible nowadays to transition and change career paths.

Going for a profession that pays more is often tempting, even if you lack the right competencies. However, it's essential to consider the long-term consequences of being in a career that doesn't align with your being. Not only will you struggle to perform well in the role, but you may also become overwhelmed, stressed, and unhappy. On the other hand, choosing a profession that aligns with your competencies and talents can lead to greater job satisfaction, a better work-life balance, and the potential for career growth and advancement. While it's important to consider salary and benefits when evaluating professions, ensuring you're a good fit for the role and that the work aligns with your personal and professional goals is equally important. To improve your chance of securing your dream job, it is vital to research the competencies, requirements, and skills expectations for your chosen profession. The specific skills that are important in a given profession can vary widely.

There are many types of online jobs that you can do from anywhere in the world, as long as you have a computer and an internet connection. Hereafter is a list of the most popular online jobs and their associated competencies to harness. The skills are listed in order of importance for each type of job. You will also observe, for instance, that time management is a competency necessary for many positions. If you don't yet know the type of position you would like to find, browse the list and see which aligns the most with your competencies. If you already have an idea, then study the requirements skills and improve on them if necessary. Don't overlook any required skills; the overall capacity to perform those skills well will define your performance in that profession. Choose your domain wisely and harness those competencies!

Accountant

An accountant is a financial professional who helps businesses and individuals manage their finances by preparing and analyzing financial statements, tracking income and expenses, and providing financial advice. They play a critical role in ensuring the accuracy and integrity of financial information.

- Accounting knowledge: A strong foundation in accounting principles, including knowledge of bookkeeping, financial statements, tax laws, and financial analysis, is necessary.

- Technical skills: Knowledge of accounting software such as QuickBooks, Xero, or Sage and familiarity with Microsoft Excel and Google Sheets is essential.

- Ethics: As an accountant, integrity and ethical behavior are critical. Online accountants must maintain confidentiality, avoid conflicts of interest, and follow ethical guidelines and principles.

- Attention to detail: Online accounting requires meticulous attention, especially when dealing with financial records and reconciliations.

- Analytical skills: Analyzing financial data and identifying trends or issues is essential for an online accountant.

- Problem-solving: Online accountants need to be able to identify and solve problems related to financial records and transactions.

- Communication skills: Strong communication skills, including the ability to explain financial concepts to clients and communicate effectively via email, phone, or video conferencing, are needed.

Content Creator

A content creator produces digital media content, such as written content, photos, graphics, and videos, for social media, websites, and other online platforms. They use their creativity and expertise to develop engaging, informative content that resonates with their target audience.

- Writing skills: The essential skill any content creator or editor should have is excellent writing skills. It's necessary to express your thoughts and ideas clearly and concisely.

- Creativity: Creativity is essential to create engaging and unique content. You need to come up with fresh ideas and think outside the box.

- Research skills: A content creator must be able to research and gather information about the topic they are writing about. This involves finding reliable sources, analyzing data, and synthesizing information.

- SEO skills: Knowing the basics of search engine optimization (SEO) is crucial to ensuring your content is discoverable by search engines and reaches a broader audience.

- Social media skills: Social media platforms are vital for content creators and bloggers to promote content, engage with their audience, and grow their following. Understanding how to use social media effectively is essential.

- Basic graphic design skills: Creating engaging and visually appealing content is crucial in today's digital landscape. Basic graphic design skills, such as using tools like Canva, can help enhance your content.

Community Manager

Community managers are responsible for building and maintaining online communities for businesses, organizations, or other groups. Some skills that can be helpful for a community manager to have include:

- Strong communication skills: Community managers should be able to communicate effectively with community members online and in person.

- Customer service skills: Community managers may be called upon to address customer complaints or inquiries, so strong customer service skills are essential.

- Marketing knowledge: Understanding marketing principles and how to apply them to building and maintaining a community can be helpful for a community manager.

- Familiarity with social media platforms: Community managers may use them to build and maintain their communities, so proficiency with these platforms is important.

- Organizational skills: Community managers may be responsible for managing events, projects, and other activities within the community, so strong organizational skills are important.

- Problem-solving skills: Community managers may be called upon to troubleshoot problems or find solutions to challenges that arise within the community.

- Time management skills: Community managers may have multiple tasks and deadlines, so good time management skills are essential.

Coordinator

A coordinator or event planner is a person who is responsible for organizing and synchronizing activities and tasks within a team or organization. To be an online event planner or coordinator, several skills are essential:

- Organization: As an event planner or coordinator, you will be responsible for organizing every aspect of an event. This requires excellent organizational skills to ensure everything runs smoothly and nothing is overlooked.

- Communication: Effective communication is crucial for successful online event planners or coordinators. You must communicate with clients, vendors, and other stakeholders to ensure everyone is on the same page and the event is executed as planned.

- Creativity: Creating unique and memorable events requires a certain level of creativity. As an event planner, you will need to come up with new ideas and be able to think outside the box to create a successful event.

- Time management: Online event planning requires excellent time management skills to ensure all tasks are completed on time and within budget. You will need to be able to prioritize tasks and manage your time effectively.

- Customer service: Good customer service skills are essential to maintain positive client relationships. You must handle any issues professionally and ensure clients are satisfied with the event.

- Attention to detail: A successful event requires attention to every detail, from the invitations to the decor to the catering. As an online event planner or coordinator, you must have a keen eye for detail to ensure everything is perfect.

Copywriting

Copywriting is creating written content for marketing and advertising purposes, such as website copy, brochures, and social media posts. If you love writing and can do research, this could be the right fit for you. Some skills that can be helpful for a copywriter to have include:

- Strong writing skills: A copywriter should be able to write clearly, concisely, and effectively, with strong attention to detail and grammar.

- Creativity: Copywriters should be able to develop original and compelling ideas for their written content.

- Research skills: A copywriter may need to research a product, service, or industry to create accurate and relevant content.

- Marketing knowledge: Understanding basic marketing principles, such as the importance of targeting a specific audience, can be helpful for a copywriter.

- SEO knowledge: Familiarity with search engine optimization (SEO) can help a copywriter create content more likely to rank highly in search engine results pages.

- Collaboration skills: A copywriter may work with a team of marketers, designers, and other professionals, so strong collaboration skills can be beneficial.

Customer Service

Customer service professionals are responsible for helping customers with inquiries, complaints, and other issues. Some of the communication mediums used are phone, chat, email, and video. Some skills that can be helpful for a customer service professional to have include:

- Customer service skills: Customer service professionals should be able to handle customer inquiries and complaints politely and professionally.

- Strong communication skills: Customer service professionals communicate effectively with customers, both in person and over the phone or through other digital channels.

- Problem-solving skills: Customer service professionals should be able to identify and resolve problems that customers may be facing.

- Time management skills: Customer service professionals may have to manage multiple customer interactions and tasks, so good time management skills are important.

- Familiarity with company products or services: Customer service professionals have a good understanding of the products or services their company offers to be able to assist customers effectively.

- Computer skills: Customer service professionals use computer programs and databases to manage customer interactions and resolve issues.

- Adaptability: Customer service professionals may have to handle various customer inquiries and issues, so adapting to new tasks and environments is essential.

Data Analyst

Data analysis is a complex and evolving field that requires a diverse set of skills. It is a job in high demand and well-paid for people with the right competencies. Some of the most critical skills for a data analyst job include the following:

- Data analysis: A data analyst should have strong analytical skills to work with large amounts of data, identify trends, and draw insights from data.

- Data visualization: Data analysts should be skilled in presenting data visually using tools like graphs, charts, and dashboards. This helps to make the data easier to understand and communicate insights to stakeholders.

- Statistical knowledge: Understanding basic statistical concepts and techniques such as probability, regression, and hypothesis testing is crucial to perform data analysis effectively.

- Programming skills: Proficiency in programming languages such as Python, SQL, and SAS are essential to manipulate data, perform complex data analysis, and automating data processing tasks.

- Data management: A data analyst must be skilled in data management, including data cleaning, data preparation, and data warehousing.

- Communication skills: Communication skills are essential to convey insights and results to non-technical stakeholders effectively. Data analysts should be able to present data clearly and concisely.

- Business knowledge: A good understanding of business operations and processes is essential for a data analyst to analyze data in context, draw relevant insights, and make informed recommendations.

- Critical thinking: A data analyst must be able to think critically and creatively to solve problems and identify opportunities for improvement.

- Attention to detail: Being detail-oriented is essential to ensure that data is accurate, consistent, and error-free.

A successful data analyst should have a combination of technical, analytical, communication, and problem-solving skills. The most compelling data analysts are those who can combine their technical expertise with business acumen to provide valuable insights to stakeholders.

eCommerce Store Manager

eCommerce store managers are responsible for managing online stores and overseeing the sale of products or services through the Internet. Some popular platforms are Shopify, Amazon, eBay, Drop-shipping, etc... Often companies will hire you to help them with order fulfillment, handling refunds, product listing, etc... Some skills that can be helpful for an eCommerce store manager to have include:

- Marketing skills: eCommerce store managers should be able to create and implement marketing strategies to promote their products or services.

- Familiarity with eCommerce platforms: eCommerce store managers are proficient with the eCommerce platforms such as Shopify or WooCommerce.

- Organizational skills: eCommerce store managers need to manage inventory, orders, and other aspects of the store efficiently.

- Time management skills: eCommerce store managers may have multiple tasks and deadlines, so good time management skills are important.

- Customer service skills: eCommerce store managers are responsible for addressing customer inquiries or complaints, so strong customer service skills are essential.

- Data analysis skills: eCommerce store managers use data and analytics to track the store's performance and make adjustments as needed.

- Creativity: eCommerce store managers should be able to develop original and effective ways to promote their products or services.

Graphic Design

Graphic designers are responsible for creating visual concepts, using computer software or by hand, for communicating ideas that inspire, inform, or captivate consumers. Becoming a great graphic designer with in-depth knowledge of Photoshop or Canva is not a skill you can learn within a matter of weeks. However, if this is your bag and you turn out to work of the highest standards, many companies won't mind where you do your job from. Some of the most critical skills for a graphic designer job include the following:

- Creativity: Graphic designers should be able to come up with original and visually appealing design ideas.

- Artistic skills: Graphic designers have a strong sense of aesthetics and be able to use color, typography, and other design elements effectively.

- Knowledge of design software: Graphic designers need to be proficient in software programs such as Adobe Photoshop, Illustrator, or InDesign.

- Time management skills: Graphic designers may have multiple projects and deadlines to manage, so good time management skills are important.

- Communication skills: Graphic designers work with clients and other team members, so strong communication skills are beneficial.

- Adaptability: Graphic designers are asked to work on various projects in different industries, so adapting to new tasks and environments is important.

Project Manager

Project managers are responsible for planning, organizing, and managing projects to ensure they are completed on time and within budget. Some skills that can be helpful for a project manager to have include:

- Time management skills: Project managers should be able to manage multiple tasks and deadlines effectively.

- Organizational skills: Project managers must create and maintain organized project plans and schedules.

- Communication skills: Project managers communicate effectively with team members, clients, and other stakeholders.

- Leadership skills: Project managers lead and motivate their team members to achieve project goals.

- Problem-solving skills: Project managers are required to identify and resolve problems that arise during a project.

- Analytical skills: Project managers should be able to analyze and use data to make informed project decisions.

- Adaptability: Project managers work on various projects in different industries, so adapting to new tasks and environments is important.

SEO (Search Engine Optimization) Expert

Search engine optimization (SEO) experts are responsible for improving the visibility and ranking of websites in search engine results pages. Every business in the world can benefit from more web traffic. You can learn the fundamentals by reading search engine journals for a vast library of guides and how-to articles on SEO. Some skills that can be helpful for an SEO expert to have included the following:

- Knowledge of SEO principles: A SEO expert should understand how search engines work and the factors that can impact a website's ranking.
- Keyword research skills: A SEO expert need to identify relevant and popular keywords and phrases to target in website content and meta tags.
- On-page optimization skills: A SEO expert must optimize a website's content, structure, and technical elements to improve its ranking.
- Off-page optimization skills: A SEO expert build high-quality backlinks and engage in other activities to improve a website's ranking.
- Analytical skills: A SEO expert should be able to use data and analytics to track the performance of SEO efforts and make adjustments as needed.
- Communication skills: A SEO expert work with diverse clients and other team members, so strong communication skills are beneficial.
- Time management skills: A SEO expert can manage multiple projects and deadlines, so good time management skills are important.

Social Media Manager

Social media managers are responsible for creating and implementing social media strategies for businesses and organizations. If you spend much of your day on Facebook or Instagram, why not use it to make money? You could manage companies' social pages or run Facebook ads. It is a great online job requiring minimal technical knowledge and can be done anywhere. Some of the most critical skills for a social media manager include the following:

- Strong communication skills: Social media managers should be able to communicate effectively with clients, team members, and followers through social media platforms.

- Marketing knowledge: Understanding marketing principles and how to apply them to social media is essential for a social media manager.

- Familiarity with social media platforms: Social media managers are proficient with the various social media platforms they work on and use them effectively to reach their target audience.

- Analytical skills: Social media managers use data and analytics to track the performance of their social media campaigns and make adjustments as needed.

- Creativity: Social media managers are demanded to develop original and compelling ideas for social media content.

Software Developer

Software developers are responsible for designing, creating, testing, and maintaining software applications. Developers are hot commodities inside and outside the tech industry, and the pay is quite lucrative. This job requires knowledge and experience, usually in specific programming languages. Except if you are a veteran in development, it is challenging to master all types of frameworks and languages used in that industry. Moreover, employers prefer people who have expertise and experience matching that niche. Select a niche market in the software landscape and focus on it. Some skills that can be helpful for a software developer to have include:

- Programming skills: Software developers should be proficient in at least one programming language, such as C++, Java, PHP, JavaScript, React, etc…

- Problem-solving skills: Software developers may be called upon to troubleshoot problems or find solutions to challenges arising during development.

- Attention to detail: Software developers must work carefully and accurately, as even small mistakes can have serious consequences.

- Collaboration skills: Software developers may work with a team of designers, project managers, and other professionals, so strong collaboration skills are beneficial.

- Familiarity with development frameworks: Developers use many frameworks to speed up the development process.

- Continuous learning: The field of software development is constantly evolving, so developers should be willing to keep learning and stay up-to-date with new technologies and best practices.

Teacher

Online teachers are responsible for delivering educational content to students through virtual platforms. The possibilities are endless, whether teaching English, conversing in Spanish, or doing lectures for universities. The more qualified you are, the more income you can generate through teaching. Some of the most important skills for an online teacher include the following:

- Strong subject matter knowledge: Online teachers should thoroughly understand the subject they are teaching and be able to explain complex concepts clearly and concisely.

- Communication skills: Online teachers communicate effectively with students and other educators through virtual platforms.

- Familiarity with educational technology: Online teachers are proficient with the tools and software used for online teaching, such as video conferencing platforms and learning management systems.

- Patience: Online teachers need to be patient and able to work with students struggling with certain concepts.

- Organizational skills: Online teachers are required to create and maintain organized lesson plans and materials.

- Adaptability: Online teachers may need to adapt to different virtual platforms and technologies and their student's needs and learning styles.

Technical Customer Service

Technical customer service professionals are responsible for helping customers with technical inquiries, complaints, and other issues related to products or services that are highly technical in nature. Although Technical customer service is very similar to the customer services position, since it requires some technical expertise, it also means less competition and better pay. Acquiring technical expertise might be wise if you already have the skillsets to do a customer services job. Some skills that can be helpful for a specialized customer service professional to have include:

- Strong communication skills: Technical customer service professionals communicate effectively with customers, both in person and over the phone or through other digital channels.

- Customer service skills: Technical customer service professionals can handle customer inquiries and complaints politely and professionally.

- Problem-solving skills: Technical customer service professionals need to identify and resolve problems that customers may be facing.

- Technical knowledge: Technical customer service professionals should have a strong understanding of the products or services they are supporting, including how they work and how to troubleshoot problems.

- Time management skills: Technical customer service professionals may have to manage multiple customer interactions and tasks, so good time management skills are important.

- Computer skills: Technical customer service professionals use computer programs and databases to manage customer interactions and resolve issues.

- Adaptability: Technical customer service professionals may have to handle various projects in diverse industries, so adapting to new tasks and environments is critical.

Translator

Translators are responsible for converting written materials from one language to another. If you are not only a skilled copywriter but are also fluent in two or more languages, translation can be a great source of income. Some skills that can be helpful for a translator to have include:

- Fluency in at least two languages: Translators are proficient in the source language (the text is written in) and the target language (the language the text is being translated into).

- Strong writing skills: Translators need to write clearly and accurately in the target language, paying attention to grammar, spelling, and punctuation.

- Cultural awareness: Translators understand the cultures of the languages they translate, as cultural references and idioms can be challenging to convey accurately from one language to another.

- Research skills: Translators may need to research specific terms or phrases to ensure accurate translations.

- Computer skills: Translators may use translation software and other tools to help them with their work, so computer proficiency is helpful.

Video Producer

A video producer is a professional who oversees video content creation from conception to completion. They manage the production team, coordinate with clients and stakeholders, and ensure that the final product meets the desired specifications and objectives.

- Technical skills: Video producers have a strong understanding of the technical aspects of video production, including camera operation, lighting, sound recording, and editing. Familiarity with video editing software such as Adobe Premiere or Final Cut Pro is also essential.

- Creativity: Video production requires creativity, from creating unique concepts and storylines to producing visually appealing shots and soundscapes. Video producers must have a creative eye and the ability to think outside the box.

- Problem-solving skills: Video production can be unpredictable, and video producers may encounter unexpected challenges during a shoot or in post-production. They need to think on their feet and come up with solutions to problems quickly.

- Marketing and business skills: To be successful as a video producer, one must have strong marketing and business skills to promote the work, network with clients, and manage budgets and contracts.
- Communication skills: Video producers communicate effectively with clients, crew members, and talent to ensure everyone is on the same page and the project moves smoothly.

Virtual Assistant

Virtual assistants (VAs) support clients remotely, often working from home or in a co-working space. If you are tech-savvy and know how to check emails, answer phone calls, do data entry, update websites, do bookkeeping, or have experience in a specific industry such as real estate, a virtual assistant position might be for you. Some skills that can be helpful for a virtual assistant to have include:

- Strong communication skills: Virtual assistants must communicate effectively with clients and team members through phone, email, and other digital platforms.
- Organizational skills: Virtual assistants may be responsible for managing schedules, making travel arrangements, and handling other administrative tasks, so strong organizational skills are essential.
- Time management skills: Virtual assistants need to manage their time effectively to meet deadlines and complete tasks efficiently.
- Computer skills: Virtual assistants should be proficient with computers and be comfortable using various software programs, such as email, productivity tools, and social media platforms.
- Adaptability: Virtual assistants may work with multiple clients and industries, so adapting to new tasks and environments is required.
- Problem-solving skills: Virtual assistants may be called upon to troubleshoot problems or solve challenges.

Web Designer

Web designers are responsible for creating the visual design of websites, including the layout, color scheme, and overall aesthetic. Some skills that can be helpful for a web designer to have include:

- Graphic design skills: Web designers should have a strong understanding of design principles, such as layout, color theory, and typography.

- HTML and CSS skills: Web designers must be proficient in HTML (HyperText Markup Language) and CSS (Cascading Style Sheets), which are used to create and style web pages.

- Familiarity with design software: Web designers use software programs such as Adobe Photoshop, Illustrator, or InDesign to create website visual elements.

- Creativity: Web designers must develop original and visually appealing design ideas.

- Attention to detail: Web designers need to work carefully and accurately, as even small mistakes can have serious consequences.

- Communication skills: Web designers work with clients and other team members, so strong communication skills are beneficial.

Solving The Puzzle

‘Life is a masterpiece, and you are the artist. Paint with boldness and passion, and create a work of art that inspires and uplifts.’ - Unknown

We have evaluated many methods to help you find your calling. The secret to solving this puzzle is not to focus solely on one piece but to draw an entire picture by putting all the pieces together.

Understanding your personality alone is not enough to figure out your dream job. Passion is essential to keep the fire going and persist in your endeavor but obviously can't stand alone. Talents make the journey smoother, but it is not enough. Mastered skills add tremendous credentials to your value proposition, but skill alone is like an empty shell. Taking each of those puzzle pieces and putting them together to form a masterpiece is the key to helping you understand yourself at a much deeper level and leading you to find your calling. It is not a one-time process either; as you grow professionally, return to your masterpiece and refine it based on your newly acquired experiences and wisdom.

Exercise

"How do you know if you're doing well in life's puzzle? When all the pieces start to fall into place."

Let's gather some of those puzzle pieces and see if we can assemble them. List your top three for each puzzle piece:

Top 3 Personality Traits:

1.

2.

3.

Top 3 Passions:

    1.

    2.

    3.

Top 3 Innate Talents:

    1.

    2.

    3.

Top 3 Mastered Competencies:

    1.

    2.

    3.

Top 3 Preferred Professions:

    1.

    2.

    3.

What is the masterpiece telling you? Do you see it? Since you now have a better idea of what you are looking for, we will look at all the different industries in the next chapter and determine which best aligns with your desires and lifestyle.

IDENTIFY YOUR INDUSTRY

"Find a job you enjoy doing, and you will never have to work a day in your life." - Mark Twain

Choosing the right industry to work in can be a crucial decision impacting your career and personal fulfillment. While it may sometimes feel like the industry you end up in is simply a result of available job opportunities, it's essential to consider which industry aligns with your passions, talents, and personality. You must research and narrow down the industries that align with your calling. Once you have narrowed it down, verify that you have the competencies and skillsets required for those positions. It will help you find a fulfilling career you can be passionate about for the long term.

This chapter will help you explore the various industries and the various job roles they offer so that you can make an informed decision about the right industry for you. If you already know the industry you want to work for, specifically review the requirements and lifestyle of that industry to prepare yourself better when applying. Remember that you can learn new competencies and acquire additional training to better prepare yourself for the job roles you are interested in. Keep in mind, though, that some sectors can adapt to online positions while others have strict constraints on location and availability.

INDUSTRY CATEGORIES

The following list of industries is not exhaustive, but it should give you a sense of the many different categories of industries. Many other sectors play essential roles in the global economy; feel free to dig deeper and find a niche that matches your preferences.

- Agriculture: This industry involves the production of food, fiber, and other goods through farming, ranching, and related activities.
- Construction: This industry involves building structures such as houses, commercial buildings, and infrastructure.

- Education: This industry provides learning and training opportunities to individuals of all ages.

- Energy: This industry produces and distributes power, including fossil fuels and renewable energy sources.

- Entertainment: This industry creates and distributes media and experiences to entertain and engage audiences.

- Financial services: This industry provides financial products and services, including banking, insurance, and investment.

- Government: This industry provides public services and manages local, state, and national public affairs.

- Healthcare: This industry involves providing medical services and products to individuals and populations.

- Information technology: This industry uses computers and related technology to process, store, and transmit information.

- Manufacturing: This industry involves the production of goods through the use of labor, machinery, and other resources.

- Mining: This industry involves the extraction of minerals and other resources from the earth.

- Nonprofit: This industry involves organizations dedicated to promoting social or environmental causes that do not operate for profit.

- Professional services: This industry involves providing specialized services, such as consulting, legal, and accounting services.

- Transportation: This industry involves the movement of people and goods through various modes of transportation, including air, land, and water.

- Tourism: This industry promotes and facilitates travel and hospitality services to visitors and tourists.

- Real estate: This industry involves the buying, selling, and managing of properties and land.

- Retail: This industry involves the sale of goods and services to consumers through various channels, including stores, online platforms, and direct sales.

FACTORS TO CONSIDER

'Don't wait for the perfect opportunity; create it.' - George Bernard Shaw

Choosing the right industry is essential for many factors; here is a list of the variable elements to consider.

- Career growth: Different industries offer different opportunities for career advancement and development. Choosing an industry that aligns with your long-term goals can help you progress in your career.

- Work culture: The culture of an industry can significantly impact your overall job satisfaction and well-being. For instance, the mining, healthcare, and finance industries have incredibly different types of personalities working in those industries. Choosing an industry with a work culture that aligns with your values and preferences can lead to a more positive and fulfilling work experience.

- Job security: Some industries are more stable and have a lower risk of job loss than others. Choosing an industry with higher job security can provide peace of mind and financial stability.

- Pay and benefits: Different industries offer different pay and benefits packages. Choosing an industry that provides a compensation package that meets your financial needs and goals is important. An accountant position in the finance industry will pay much differently than an accountant in the nonprofit sector.

- Location: Some industries are more geographically concentrated than others. Choosing an industry with a strong presence in the area where you want to live can make it easier to find job opportunities. In some sectors, almost all positions can be done online, for instance, information technology, whereas other industries like mining or manufacturing require to be at a specific location.

- Work-life balance: Different industries have different demands on time and energy. For instance, the healthcare industry might have a tough schedule, whereas the retail sector has more standard office hours. Choosing an industry that allows for a good work-life balance can help you maintain a healthy and fulfilling personal life.

- Personal interests: If you have a strong passion or interest in a particular industry, choosing a job in that industry can be rewarding and fulfilling.

- Personal values: If you have strong personal values or beliefs, choosing an industry that aligns with those values can be personally satisfying and meaningful.

- Industry outlook: Some industries are growing and expanding, while others are declining. Choosing an industry with a positive outlook can increase your chances of finding job opportunities and advancing your career.

- Professional development: Different industries offer different opportunities for professional development and learning. Choosing an industry that provides opportunities for growth and advancement can help you stay up-to-date and competitive in your field.

- Knowledge and education: Some industries require constant learning and evolution of methodologies, like information technology, whereas other sectors are much more traditional, like agriculture and mining. In an industry that requires continuous adaptation and learning, youth is valued. As you age, you will need to rise to some management level or risk being outdated. In more traditional sectors, age is valued as wisdom.

- Flexibility: Some industries require vast knowledge to build experiences, and others almost none. That experience can take much time to acquire, making a change of sector a high commitment and challenging endeavor.

INDUSTRY SPECIFICS

Choosing the right industry for your job is crucial because it can impact many aspects of your career and personal life. Don't blindly jump on the first job offer you get. Consider your goals, values, and preferences before working in a specific industry. In this section, we list many industries and explain the advantages, constraints, and drawbacks so that you can make an informed decision.

Agriculture

"Agriculture is our wisest pursuit because it will, in the end, contribute most to real wealth, good morals, and happiness." - Thomas Jefferson

Agriculture refers to producing and distributing food, fiber, and other products from plants and animals. It includes various activities, such as farming, ranching, forestry, and fishing. Some key agricultural industry players include farmers, ranchers, and forestry workers. The agriculture industry can have a significant impact on local and global economies. It can be a primary source of employment for people in a wide range of fields, including farming, ranching, forestry, and food processing. Agriculture is closely linked to the transportation and food processing industries, as agricultural products are usually transported and processed for distribution.

Here are some of the general characteristics of the work culture in the agriculture industry:

- Physical work: The agriculture industry often involves physically demanding work, such as working with heavy machinery or lifting and carrying heavy loads.

- Seasonal work: Many jobs in the agriculture industry are seasonal, with busy times during planting and harvesting seasons and slower times during other parts of the year.

- Outdoor work: The agriculture industry regularly involves working outside, regardless of the weather.

- <u>Attention to detail</u>: The agriculture industry requires attention to detail, as farmers and other agriculture workers must pay close attention to the health and well-being of their crops and animals.

- <u>Flexibility</u>: The agriculture industry requires flexibility and the ability to adapt to changing circumstances, such as weather or market conditions.

- <u>Extended hours</u>: The agriculture industry can involve long hours, particularly during busy seasons.

- <u>Rural location</u>: Many jobs in the agriculture industry are located in rural areas, which can be a unique aspect of the work environment.

- <u>Connectedness to the land</u>: Working in the agriculture industry can give you a sense of connection to the land and the environment.

- <u>Economic instability</u>: The agriculture industry can be subject to fluctuations in prices and demand, which can impact the stability of farming businesses.

Construction

'Construction is not about hammers and nails; it's about people and their dreams.' - Anonymous

The construction industry refers to building and repairing structures, such as buildings, bridges, roads, and infrastructure. It includes various activities like design, development, construction, and maintenance. Some key players in the construction industry include contractors, engineers, and construction workers. The construction industry can have a significant impact on local and global economies. It is a primary source of employment for people in a wide range of fields, including construction, engineering, and architecture. The construction industry is closely linked to the real estate and manufacturing industries, as construction projects often require materials and equipment that manufacturers produce.

Here are some general characteristics of the work culture in the construction industry:

- <u>Physical work</u>: The construction industry often involves physically demanding work, such as lifting and carrying heavy materials or working with hand tools.

- Teamwork: The construction industry involves working in teams, each member contributing to the building or renovation process.

- Attention to detail: The construction industry requires attention to detail, as buildings and structures need to be built to precise specifications.

- Weather-related challenges: Construction work can be disrupted or delayed by weather events like rain or extreme heat.

- Safety: The construction industry strongly emphasizes safety, with strict guidelines and protocols to protect workers from accidents and injuries.

- Deadlines: The construction industry requires meeting deadlines, as construction projects often have a set completion date.

- Extended hours: The construction industry can involve long hours, mainly when working on a project with a tight schedule.

- Adaptability: The construction industry is subject to changes in project scope, schedules, and budgets, so it's essential to be adaptable and able to work under pressure.

- Technical skills: The construction industry requires specialized skills and knowledge, such as reading and interpreting blueprints or using construction equipment.

Education

'Education is the most powerful weapon which you can use to change the world.' - Nelson Mandela

The education industry refers to providing education and training to people of all ages. It includes various activities, such as primary and secondary education, higher education, and vocational training. Some key players in the education industry include schools, universities, and training institutions. The education industry can have a significant impact on local and global economies. The education industry is often closely linked to other sectors, as many businesses and organizations rely on education and training to develop the skills and knowledge of their employees.

Here are some general characteristics of the work culture in the education industry:

- Collaborative: The education industry often involves working with a wide range of people, including teachers, students, administrators, and support staff; hence working well in a team is necessary.

- Student-centered: The education industry is often student-centered, focusing on providing students with a positive and supportive learning environment.

- Professional development: The education industry strongly emphasizes professional development and continuous learning. Teachers and other education professionals must stay current on the latest research and best practices.

- Flexibility: The education industry requires flexibility and the ability to adapt to changing circumstances, such as changes in curriculum or student needs.

- Empathy: The education industry involves working with students with diverse needs and learning styles, so compassion and understanding are essential.

- Long hours: The education industry can involve extended hours, particularly for teachers, who may have to prepare lessons, grade papers, and meet with students outside regular class time.

- Personal satisfaction: Some people find personal joy in their work, particularly in helping students learn and grow.

- Public service: Many people in the education industry see their work as a form of public service, focusing on helping students succeed and reach their potential.

- High expectations: The education industry often has high expectations for teachers and other professionals responsible for helping students learn and grow.

Energy

'Energy is the golden thread that connects economic growth, social equity, and environmental sustainability.' - Ban Ki-moon

The energy industry refers to producing and distributing energy, such as electricity, natural gas, and fuel. It includes various activities, such as exploration, extraction, production, and distribution. Some key players in the energy industry include energy companies, engineers, and energy workers. The energy industry can have a significant impact on local and global economies. It is a primary source of employment for people in the fields such as engineering, production, and distribution. The energy industry is often linked to mining, transportation, and manufacturing. Many energy sources require raw materials extracted from the earth and transported to energy production facilities.

Here are some general characteristics of the work culture in the energy industry:

- Teamwork: The energy industry involves working in teams, with each team member contributing to the production or distribution of energy.

- Safety: The energy industry strongly emphasizes safety, with strict guidelines and protocols to protect workers from accidents and injuries.

- Attention to detail: The energy industry requires attention, as energy products and systems must be maintained and operated precisely.

- Shift work: Many jobs in the energy industry involve shift work, with different teams working different shifts to keep the energy production or distribution operation running around the clock.

- Physical fitness: Some jobs in the energy industry may involve physically demanding tasks or working in challenging environments.

- Long hours: The energy industry can involve extended hours, mainly when working on a project with a tight schedule.

- Technical skills: The energy industry often requires specialized skills and knowledge, such as operating machinery or computer-aided design software.

- Environmental concerns: The energy industry is closely linked to environmental concerns, as energy production and use can impact the environment. Many energy industry companies focus on developing and implementing sustainable energy solutions.

Entertainment

"Entertainment is a form of art that can bring people together and create lasting memories." - Beyoncé

The entertainment industry produces and distributes media and cultural products, such as movies, television shows, music, and live performances. It includes various activities, from creating and delivering content to distributing and promoting it to audiences. Some key players in the entertainment industry have film studios, television networks, music labels, and theater companies. The entertainment industry can significantly impact popular culture and be a significant source of employment for people in creative and technical fields.

Here are some general characteristics of the work culture in the entertainment industry:

- Fast-paced: The entertainment industry is fast-paced and deadline-driven, particularly in film and television.

- Creative: The entertainment industry is a place for creativity and innovation, focusing on developing and producing new, engaging content.

- Stress: The entertainment industry can be stressful, mainly when working under tight deadlines or performing in front of a live audience.

- Collaborative: The entertainment industry involves working with a wide range of people, including writers, actors, directors, and producers, so it's essential to work well in a team.

- Unpredictable: The entertainment industry can be unpredictable, with projects and schedules often changing at the last minute.

- Highly competitive: The entertainment industry is highly competitive, with many talented people vying for a limited number of jobs.

- Persistence: The entertainment industry is competitive, so it's essential to be persistent and resilient in the face of rejection.

- Extended hours: The entertainment industry can involve long hours, mainly when working on a project with a tight deadline.

- Variety of job roles: The entertainment industry offers various roles, from hands-on, creative positions to management roles.

- Adaptability: The entertainment industry is subject to changes in market demand and trends, so it's essential to be adaptable and learn new skills.

- Unique work environment: The entertainment industry has a unique work environment, depending on the type of company or organization. For example, a film studio might have a more formal work environment, while a music venue might have a more laid-back atmosphere.

Financial Services

"Financial services are the lifeblood of commerce and business, and it has a direct impact on people's lives." - Sallie Krawcheck

The financial services industry refers to providing financial products and services to individuals, businesses, and organizations. It includes activities like banking, investment, insurance, and financial planning. Some of the key players in the financial services industry include banks, investment firms, and financial advisors. The financial services industry significantly impacts local and global economies. It is a source of employment for people in various fields, including finance, accounting, and banking. The financial services industry is often linked to other sectors, as businesses and organizations rely on financial services to help them manage their financial resources.

Here are some general characteristics of the work culture in the financial services industry:

- Professionalism: The financial services industry emphasizes professionalism, maintaining strict ethical standards, and providing high-quality service to clients.
- Good pay: Many jobs in the financial services industry offer good pay and benefits packages.
- Stress: The financial services industry can be stressful, particularly when working under tight deadlines or dealing with complex financial cases.
- Fast-paced: The financial services industry is fast-paced, focusing on meeting deadlines and staying up-to-date with the latest developments in the field.
- Attention to detail: The financial services industry requires attention to detail, as financial transactions and records need to be accurately processed and tracked.
- Communication skills: The financial services industry often involves working with a diverse range of people, so it's important to have good communication skills.

- Technical skills: The financial services industry requires specialized skills and knowledge, such as financial analysis or accounting software.

- Lifelong learning: The financial services industry is constantly evolving, so it's essential to be open to learning new technologies and skills.

- Competition for jobs: The financial services industry can be competitive, with many qualified candidates vying for a limited number of jobs.

- Flexibility: The financial services industry often requires flexibility and the ability to adapt to changing circumstances, such as regulations or market conditions.

Government

"The government is us; we are the government, you and I." - Theodore Roosevelt

The government refers to the institutions and agencies responsible for the administration and regulation of a country or region. This includes national governments, as well as state, local, and regional governments. The government industry is responsible for various activities, including policy-making, law enforcement, tax collection, and public services such as healthcare, education, and infrastructure. Some key players in the government industry include elected officials, civil servants, and various agencies and departments responsible for specific areas of policy and regulation. The government significantly impacts citizens' lives and employs people in a wide range of fields.

Here are some general characteristics of the work culture in the government industry:

- Teamwork: The government involves working in teams, with each team member contributing to the success of the agency or organization.

- Guarantee of employment: Most governments offer a guarantee of employment for a lifetime.

- Lower pay: Usually, government positions are expected to pay less than the equivalent positions in the private sector.

- Service to the community: The government often involves serving the community's needs, whether providing social services, enforcing laws and regulations, or managing public resources.

- Bureaucracy: The government can involve bureaucracy, focusing on following established policies and procedures and obtaining necessary approvals before taking action.

Healthcare

'The greatest wealth is health.' - Virgil

The healthcare industry refers to providing medical and health-related products and services to people. It includes various activities, such as diagnosis, treatment, and prevention of diseases and injuries. Some of the key players in the healthcare industry include hospitals, clinics, and healthcare professionals. It can be a major source of employment for people in a wide range of fields, including medicine, nursing, and healthcare administration. Healthcare is closely linked to the pharmaceutical and insurance industries, as many products and services require medication and insurance coverage.

Here are some general characteristics of the work culture in the healthcare industry:

- Patient-centered: The healthcare industry is patient-centered. It focuses on providing high-quality care and patient support.

- Safety: The healthcare industry emphasizes safety, with strict guidelines and protocols to protect patients and healthcare workers from accidents and injuries.

- Communication skills: The healthcare industry involves working with a diverse range of people, so it's essential to have good communication skills.

- Extended hours: The healthcare industry can involve long hours, particularly for healthcare professionals who work in hospitals or other facilities that provide 24-hour care.

- Attention to detail: The healthcare industry requires attention to detail, as the well-being of patients is at stake.

- Education and training: Many jobs in the healthcare industry require specialized education and training, such as a degree in nursing, medicine, or therapy.

- Professional development: The healthcare industry highlights professional development and continuous learning, as healthcare professionals are expected to stay up-to-date on the latest research and best practices in their field.

- Stress: The healthcare industry can be stressful, particularly when working under tight deadlines or dealing with complex medical cases.

- Emotional labor: The healthcare industry often involves emotional labor, as healthcare professionals need to be compassionate and supportive to patients and their families, even in difficult or stressful situations.

Information Technology

"The most profound technologies are those that disappear. They weave themselves into the fabric of everyday life until they are indistinguishable from it." - Mark Weiser

The information technology (IT) industry refers to the business of designing, developing, and providing technology-related products and services. It includes various activities like software development, hardware design, and IT consulting. Some key players in the IT industry include technology companies, software developers, and IT professionals. It provides employment for people in computer science, engineering, and design. The IT industry is always connected to other industries, as most businesses and organizations rely on IT products and services to operate more efficiently and effectively.

Here are some general characteristics of the work culture in the information technology (IT) industry:

- Fast-paced: The IT industry is fast-paced. It focuses on meeting deadlines and staying up-to-date with the latest technologies.

- Problem-solving skills: The IT industry involves solving complex technical problems, so it's essential to have strong problem-solving skills.

- Collaborative: The IT industry requires working with a wide range of people, including software developers, IT professionals, and end users, so it's essential to work well in a team.

- Technical skills: The IT industry entails specialized skills and knowledge, such as programming languages or networking concepts.

- Attention to detail: The IT industry necessitates attention to detail, as technology systems must be designed and implemented precisely.

- Competition for jobs: The IT industry can be competitive, with many qualified candidates vying for a limited number of jobs.

- Lifelong learning: The IT industry is constantly evolving, so it's essential to be open to learning new technologies and skills.

- Stress: The IT industry can be stressful, particularly when working under tight deadlines or dealing with complex technical problems.

- Flexibility: The IT industry requires flexibility and the ability to adapt to changing circumstances, such as new software releases or changes in business needs.

Manufacturing

'Manufacturing is more than just putting parts together. It's coming up with ideas, testing principles, and perfecting the engineering, as well as final assembly.' - James Dyson

The manufacturing industry produces automobiles, appliances, clothing, and electronics. It includes various activities, such as design, development, production, and distribution. Some of the key players in the manufacturing industry include manufacturers, engineers, and production workers. It is a significant source of employment in many regions for people in various fields, including engineering, production, and logistics. The manufacturing industry is directly linked to the transportation and distribution industries, as manufactured goods are often transported and distributed to customers.

Here are some general characteristics of the work culture in the manufacturing industry:

- Variety of job roles: The manufacturing industry offers various job roles, from technical positions to management roles.

- Safety: The manufacturing industry strongly emphasizes safety, with strict guidelines and protocols to protect workers from accidents and injuries.

- Teamwork: The manufacturing industry involves working in teams, each member contributing to the production process.

- Opportunities for advancement: The manufacturing industry offers promotion and professional development opportunities.

- Production goals: The manufacturing industry has production goals that need to be met, which can create a sense of pressure to work efficiently.

- Shift work: Many jobs in the manufacturing industry involve shift work, with different teams working different shifts to keep the production line running around the clock.

- Long hours: The manufacturing industry can involve extended hours, particularly when meeting production deadlines or when working on a project with a tight schedule.

- Technical skills: The manufacturing industry necessitates technical skills and knowledge, such as operating machinery or computer-aided design software.

- Good pay: Many jobs in the manufacturing industry offer good pay and benefits packages.

- Attention to detail: The manufacturing industry often requires attention to detail, as products need to be made to precise specifications.

Mining

"Mining is a vital industry that contributes to the economic growth and development of countries around the world." - Anthony Albanese

The mining industry refers to extracting minerals and other raw materials from the earth. It includes various activities, such as exploration, extraction, processing, and transportation. Some of the key players in the mining industry include mining companies, engineers, and miners. The mining industry can have a significant impact on local and global economies. It can be a primary source of employment for people in a wide range of fields, including geology, engineering, and mining. The mining industry is often closely linked to the manufacturing and energy industries, as many raw materials extracted from the earth produce a wide range of products and fuels.

Here are some general characteristics of the work culture in the mining industry:

- <u>Physical work</u>: The mining industry involves physically demanding work, such as operating heavy machinery or working in underground mines.

- <u>Safety risks</u>: The mining industry can present certain safety risks, and workers need to follow safety protocols and use protective equipment to reduce the risk of injury.

- <u>Remote locations</u>: Many jobs in the mining industry are located in remote areas, which can be a unique aspect of the work environment.

- <u>Shift work</u>: Lots of jobs in the mining industry involve shift work, with different teams working different shifts to keep the mining operation running around the clock.

- <u>Environmental concerns</u>: The mining industry can negatively impact the environment through pollution and habitat destruction.

- <u>Teamwork</u>: The mining industry requires working in teams, each member contributing to the mining process.

- <u>Extended hours</u>: The mining industry can involve long hours, mainly when working on a project with a tight schedule.

- <u>Technical skills</u>: The mining industry often requires specialized skills and knowledge, such as operating machinery or computer-aided design software.

Nonprofit

"Nonprofits are the change makers, the problem solvers, and the visionaries that make our communities stronger." - Jacqueline Novogratz

The nonprofit industry refers to organizations that promote a specific cause or mission rather than generate profits for shareholders. Nonprofits can participate in various activities, such as education, healthcare, the arts, social services, and environmental conservation. Some key players in the nonprofit industry include charities, foundations, and advocacy groups. The nonprofit sector employs people in fields like social work, education, fundraising, and marketing. Nonprofits often rely on donations and grants to fund their activities, and volunteers run many.

Here are some general characteristics of the work culture in the nonprofit industry:

- <u>Communication skills</u>: The nonprofit industry involves working with a diverse range of people, so it's essential to have good communication skills.

- <u>Professionalism</u>: The nonprofit industry promotes professionalism, maintaining strict ethical standards and providing high-quality service to clients or beneficiaries.

- <u>Service to the community</u>: The nonprofit industry involves serving the community's needs, whether providing social services, advocating for social justice, or supporting environmental conservation efforts.

- <u>Personal satisfaction</u>: Many people find joy in their work in the nonprofit industry, particularly in helping promote a cause they believe in.

- <u>Emotional labor</u>: The nonprofit industry involves emotional labor, as nonprofit professionals must be compassionate and supportive to clients or beneficiaries, even in difficult or stressful situations.

- <u>Flexibility</u>: The nonprofit industry requires flexibility and the ability to adapt to changing circumstances, such as shifts in funding or changes in community needs.

Professional Services

"The professional services industry is built on trust, expertise, and relationships." - Gabe Larsen

The professional services industry refers to providing specialized services to businesses and organizations. This includes consulting, legal services, accounting, and engineering activities. Some of the key players in the professional services industry include consulting firms, law firms, accounting firms, and engineering firms. The professional services industry employs people in various fields, including business, law, finance, and engineering. The professional services industry is linked to other sectors, as businesses and organizations rely on these services to help them operate more efficiently and effectively.

Here are some general characteristics of the work culture in the professional services industry:

- Communication skills: The professional services industry requires working with a diverse range of people, so it's vital to have good communication skills.

- Time management: The professional services industry necessitates strong time management skills, as professionals must juggle multiple tasks and clients simultaneously.

- Attention to detail: The professional services industry requires attention to detail, as professional services are often highly specialized and require a high level of expertise.

- Professionalism: The professional services industry emphasizes professionalism, maintaining strict ethical standards, and providing high-quality service to clients.

- Fast-paced: The professional services industry is fast-paced, focusing on meeting deadlines and staying up-to-date with the latest developments in the field.

- Lifelong learning: The professional services industry is constantly evolving, so it's essential to be open to learning new technologies and skills.

- Flexibility: The professional services industry often requires flexibility and the ability to adapt to changing circumstances, such as client needs shifts or industry regulations.

Transportation

"Transportation is an essential component of a modern, thriving society." - Norman Y. Mineta

The transportation industry refers to transporting people, goods, and materials from one place to another. It includes activities such as air, land, and sea transportation. Some key players in the transportation industry include transportation companies, pilots, drivers, and workers. The transportation industry can have a significant impact on local and global economies. It is a source of employment for people in a wide range of fields, including transportation, logistics, and engineering. The transportation industry relates to many other sectors, as transporting goods and materials is essential for many businesses and organizations.

Here are some general characteristics of the work culture in the transportation industry:

- Safety: The transportation industry emphasizes safety, with strict guidelines and protocols to protect workers and passengers from accidents and injuries.

- Attention to detail: The transportation industry requires attention to detail, as transportation systems and vehicles must be maintained and operated precisely.

- Shift work: Many jobs in the transportation industry involve shift work, with different teams working different shifts to keep the transportation system running around the clock.

- Long hours: The transportation industry can involve extended hours, mainly when working on a project with a tight schedule.

- Customer service: The transportation industry can involve customer service, as transportation companies are responsible for helping passengers to get to their destinations safely and comfortably.

- Economic instability: The transportation industry can be subject to fluctuations in demand and competition, impacting job security and stability.

- Physical work: The transportation industry can involve a physically demanding job, depending on the specific role or position. For example, a truck driver might need to lift and carry heavy loads, while a public transit operator might need to drive a bus or train.

Tourism

'Tourism is a way to bring the world closer together and to promote understanding between different cultures and peoples.' - Taleb Rifai

The tourism industry refers to providing travel and hospitality services to tourists. It includes activities such as transportation, accommodation, dining, and entertainment. Some of the key players in the tourism industry include hotels, airlines, restaurants, and tour operators. The tourism industry can have a significant impact on local economies. It is a source of employment for people in hospitality, travel, and customer service. Tourism is closely linked to the transportation and entertainment industries, as tourists rely on these services to travel and experience new destinations.

Here are some general characteristics of the work culture in the tourism industry:

- Customer service: The tourism industry requires outstanding customer service, as tourism companies are responsible for helping travelers to plan and enjoy their vacations or business trips.

- Fast-paced: The tourism industry is fast-paced, focusing on meeting deadlines and providing efficient service to travelers on minute notice.

- Communication skills: The tourism industry necessitates working with a diverse range of people, so it's crucial to have good communication skills.

- Flexibility: The tourism industry often requires flexibility and the ability to adapt to changing circumstances, such as travel plans or customer demand shifts. It is also subject to market demand and trends changes, so it's important to be adaptable and learn new skills.

- Irregular work schedule: Many jobs in the tourism industry involve irregular work schedules, including long hours and overnight shifts.

Real Estate

"Real estate agents don't sell houses; they sell dreams." - unknown

The real estate industry involves buying, selling, and developing properties like homes, offices, and commercial buildings. It includes various activities, such as property management, appraisal, and financing. Some key players in the real estate industry include agents, brokers, property developers, and investment trusts. The real estate industry can have a significant impact on local economies. The real estate industry is closely linked to the construction industry, as the development of new properties usually requires the construction of new buildings.

Here are some general characteristics of the work culture in the real estate industry:

- Communication skills: The real estate industry involves working with a diverse range of people, so it's crucial to have good communication skills.

- Sales skills: Many jobs in the real estate industry involve selling properties, so it's vital to have good sales skills.

- Fast-paced: The real estate industry is often fast-paced, focusing on meeting deadlines and staying up-to-date with the latest developments in the field.

- Flexibility: The real estate industry requires flexibility and the ability to adapt to changing circumstances, such as market conditions or client needs.

- Time management: The real estate industry requires strong time management skills, as real estate professionals must be able to juggle multiple tasks and clients simultaneously.

- Attention to detail: The real estate industry requires attention to detail, as transactions involve complex legal documents and financial agreements.

- Professionalism: The real estate industry often strongly emphasizes professionalism, maintaining strict ethical standards, and providing high-quality service to clients.

Retail

"Retail is not just about selling things; it's about creating an experience. It's about building a relationship with your customers that goes beyond the transaction." - Ron Johnson

The retail industry refers to selling goods and services directly to consumers. It includes various activities, such as retail sales, marketing, and customer service. Some key players in the retail industry include retail stores, online retailers, and salespeople. The retail sector can have a significant impact on local and global economies. It can be a major source of employment for people in a wide range of fields, including sales, marketing, and customer service.

Here are some general characteristics of the work culture in the retail industry:

- Customer service: The retail industry requires excellent customer service skills, as retailers are responsible for helping customers to find the products they need and providing them with a positive shopping experience.

- Shift work: Many jobs in the retail industry involve shift work, with different teams working different shifts to keep the store open during business hours.

- Long hours: The retail industry can involve extended hours, particularly during busy seasons or when working on a project with a tight schedule.

- Fast-paced: The retail industry is often fast-paced, focusing on meeting sales goals and providing efficient service to customers.

- Flexibility: The retail industry often requires flexibility and the ability to adapt to changing circumstances, such as customer demand changes, shifts in in-store policies, and seasonal demands.

- Attention to detail: The retail industry often requires attention to detail, as products must be organized and appealing to customers.

Now that we reviewed some industries and listed essential factors to consider for each of them. Consider what is important to you and what you want to achieve in your career. Review your values, skills, and interests and how they might align with different industries.

Start exploring different industries to get a sense of what they are like and what they offer. Look for industry-specific resources and websites, attend industry events and job fairs, and talk to people who work in different industries to learn more. Discuss with family, friends, or even industry experts to find out what it is like to work in those industries. Consider what jobs you might be qualified for and which industries might be a good fit for your skills and experience. Look for job openings in industries that interest you to understand what types of roles are available and what employers are looking for.

Exercise

"What do you call an industry that specializes in making long-lasting chocolate? The cocoa-nut industry!"

List the top three industries you would like to work in and why?

1.

2.

3.

Similarly, list the top three industries you don't want to work for and why?

1.

2.

3.

LOCATE YOUR HUNTING GROUND

"If you don't go after what you want, you'll never have it. If you don't ask, the answer is always no. If you don't step forward, you're always in the same place." - Nora Roberts

Now that you have a clearer idea of what kind of job you want, let's figure out where to find such a position. There are numerous places to find jobs. Each country or city has its way of advertising jobs to the local population. We leave it to you to find places where local businesses advertise their open positions. Seek local newspapers' websites, job forums, local advertising avenues, or even directly to the website of those local organizations.

This chapter will focus on how you find a job online. Those companies might be in another city or even in another country. If you apply for a company in a different country, you must consider two things. The spoken language and the time zone for you to work in such an organization might require work at night or other flexible hours. You also need to realize that holidays might differ significantly from your local tradition, so do not expect them to respect your local holidays.

There are online jobs for any industry and any level of hierarchy. More and more companies are willing to have even their top-level managers work remotely. However, some jobs cannot be executed remotely, but even for those jobs, the hiring process usually starts on a website. It is interesting to remember that two-thirds of employment are with companies with less than 100 employees. Although working with a well-known organization might be enticing, do not overlook small companies or startups. Additionally, since smaller organizations are more flexible, finding a beneficial arrangement for both parties might be more accessible.

Focus and prioritizing are crucial when hunting for a job because they help you maximize your time and energy. Job hunting can be daunting and overwhelming, with countless job postings, applications, and interviews. It can be attractive to send as many applications as possible in the hope that you lend something. That strategy rarely works. By focusing on the types of jobs that align with your skills, interests, and career goals, you can avoid wasting time on irrelevant opportunities and increase your chances of finding a job that genuinely excites you. Do not hesitate to pass on an average job posting. Prioritizing your job search means focusing on the most promising leads and allocating your resources (such as time, money, and effort) accordingly. By being intentional and strategic about your job search, you can avoid burnout and stay motivated, even in the face of eventual rejection or setbacks.

There are two main avenues to getting a job in a specific organization. The most common and traditional will be to apply for a job offer from that company. Another way would be to become a fan of that organization, participate in their social media discussions, and make yourself visible to the organization online or onsite during events and conferences. There are many social media avenues; some of the most common are Facebook groups, Telegram channels, Discord servers, Instagram, etc... As you contribute to those social media avenues, organizations might pick up on your commitment and approach you with an offer. At least you can approach them with much more conviction since you have proven contribution and commitment.

If you have a specific company in mind that you would like to work for, one key point is knowing as much as possible about that organization. Refer to the "Know Them Better Than They Do" chapter to learn how to become an expert on a specific company.

WHERE TO FIND ONLINE JOBS

"Don't watch the clock; do what it does. Keep going." - Sam Levenson

Whether you want to be a teacher, virtual assistant, or manager, here's a list of online job boards and companies to help you find online work opportunities.

The key to most online job websites is to develop an attractive profile. The main problem with online jobs is trust. Academic accomplishment is irrelevant because people are unfamiliar with your local schools and universities. Even validating experience is not as easy as when you apply to a local company. To compensate for that, job websites provide a history of your work and feedback for previous jobs on that platform. This has another implication, building a profile might take a little while. It also means you can't develop a profile on too many job platforms since you must complete actual jobs. Hence it is essential to choose the right platform for the job you are looking for and want to grow into in the longer term. Whether new to the platform or a seasoned freelancer, following best practices can help you stand out and attract potential clients.

The first step is to complete your profile. Ensure your profile is professional-looking, complete, and accurately showcases your skills and experience. Use a high-quality profile picture and ensure that your language and tone are appropriate for the platform and the jobs you're applying for. By presenting yourself professionally and polishedly, you increase your credibility and make a positive first impression on potential clients.

Next, it's essential to highlight your skills and experiences in a way relevant to the jobs you're applying for. Use keywords commonly used in job postings to make it easier for clients to find you, and focus on showcasing your strengths and unique selling points. Additionally, consider taking skills tests offered by the platform to demonstrate your expertise in specific areas. Completing relevant tests and earning high scores can boost your profile and make you more attractive to potential clients.

If you're new to the platform, consider starting with smaller jobs to build your reputation and earn positive reviews. This can help establish your credibility and increase your chances of being hired for more extensive and lucrative projects in the future. However, it's essential to be selective when applying for jobs. Only apply for jobs that you're truly qualified for, and that match your skills and experience. Avoid applying for jobs you're not a good fit for, as this can hurt your reputation and make it harder to attract future clients.

When submitting proposals for jobs, make sure to customize each bid to highlight how your skills and experience match the job's specific requirements. Avoid submitting generic proposals or templates, as these can be impersonal and unprofessional. Additionally, be responsive and communicate clearly and professionally with clients. Respond to messages and requests promptly and keep clients updated on your progress. Demonstrating reliability and professionalism can increase your chances of being hired for the job.

Finally, it's essential to focus on building relationships with clients. Treat each client as an opportunity to build a long-term relationship. Provide excellent service and high-quality work to increase your chances of being hired or recommended for future jobs. By building solid and positive relationships with clients, you can establish yourself as a reliable and trusted freelancer and increase your chances of success on the platform.

In conclusion, finding work on job platforms requires effective communication and relationship-building strategies. By following these tips and best practices, you can increase your chances of success and position yourself as a valuable and in-demand freelancer.

JOBS PLATFORMS & LISTINGS

We cannot understate how important it is to choose the right platform for the kind of position and industry you are choosing. The following list identifies the most popular platforms, study them and choose one wisely. Remember, you must build an enticing profile for each of them. It takes time and commitment.

Linkedin Jobs

https://www.linkedin.com/jobs

LinkedIn is a social networking platform designed for professionals and businesses. Its primary purpose is to help people connect with other professionals and build their professional network.

LinkedIn is a powerful tool for job seekers, allowing them to search and apply for job openings, research companies, and connect with recruiters and hiring managers.

A more extensive LinkedIn network can benefit a user's career and professional development. It can provide access to new job opportunities, help build relationships with other professionals in the same field, and increase visibility and credibility in the industry.

Job opportunities on LinkedIn are usually long-term contracts. If you want to build a career in the professional world, an active LinkedIn profile is an important asset.

Upwork

https://www.upwork.com

Upwork provides a platform for businesses to hire talented freelancers and for freelancers to find work and build their careers. The platform has various freelance job categories, including programming, web development, design, writing, marketing, and customer service.

Upwork charges a fee for its services, depending on the project size and the payment method. The platform takes a percentage of the freelancer's earnings as a commission fee and charges businesses a processing fee for each payment.

On UpWork, you will find long-term or short-term contracts; although there is much competition on each job offer, and usually, to get a long-term contract, you must have a history of previous successful jobs on UpWork. Building your profile would require working on short-term contracts at a lower rate.

Freelancer

https://www.freelancer.com

Freelancers advertise themselves as the World's largest freelance marketplace. It offers a wide range of functionality and features for businesses to hire talented freelancers, find work, and build their careers. Freelancer offers membership-based plans and generally has lower fees than Upwork.

Fiverr

https://www.fiverr.com

Fiverr is an online freelance marketplace that connects businesses and individuals with freelancers and independent professionals for various projects and tasks.

One unique aspect of Fiverr is that it allows freelancers to offer their services in "gigs," which are fixed-price services that clients can purchase. Gigs can range in price from $5 to hundreds or even thousands of dollars, depending on the service's complexity and the freelancer's experience.

Remote Jobs Club

https://remotejobsclub.com

Remote Jobs Club is a job board and newsletter that curates and shares remote job opportunities from various sources, including company websites, job boards, and social media platforms.

The goal of RemoteJobsClub.com is to make it easier for people to find and apply for remote jobs by aggregating job postings from multiple sources and delivering them to subscribers' inboxes every week. The newsletter includes a curated list of remote job opportunities in various fields, including software development, marketing, customer support, design, and more.

Remote Jobs Club is free to use for both job seekers and employers.

SkipTheDrive

https://www.skipthedrive.com/

SkipTheDrive is a job board and remote job aggregator that specializes in providing remote job opportunities for job seekers looking to work from home or anywhere around the world.

SkipTheDrive aims to help job seekers find legitimate remote job opportunities by curating job postings from various sources, including company websites, job boards, and social media platforms. The website features remote job listings in multiple categories, including customer service, marketing, sales, software development, and more.

SkipTheDrive is free for job seekers, and employers can post job listings for a fee.

We Work Remotely

https://weworkremotely.com/

We Work Remotely is a remote job board that features job listings for remote positions in various fields, including software development, marketing, customer support, design, and more.

The website features remote job listings from companies of all sizes, from startups to large corporations. It allows job seekers to search for remote jobs based on their preferred job category, location, and keyword.

We Work Remotely is known for its high-quality job listings and the vetting process to ensure that only legitimate remote job opportunities are posted on the website. The website charges a fee for employers to post job listings, which helps to ensure that the job listings are high-quality and legitimate.

Remote.Co

https://remote.co/

Remote Work is a job board and resource hub that provides remote job opportunities and resources for job seekers seeking remote work.

The goal of Remote.co is to make it easier for job seekers to find legitimate remote job opportunities by curating job postings from various sources and delivering them to job seekers' inboxes every week.

Remote.co is free for job seekers, and employers can post job listings for a fee.

FlexJobs

https://www.flexjobs.com/

FlexJobs list high-quality online, work-from-home, and flexible jobs in 50+ career categories; our goal is to provide you with a top-notch job search experience.

Wellfound

https://angel.co/

Wellfound makes it easy to find your dream job - regardless of location. Browse over 100,000 jobs, from top companies to fast-growing startups.

Remote Ok

https://remoteok.com/

Remote OK has online jobs as a Developer, Designer, Copywriter, Customer Support Rep, Sales Professional, Project Manager, and more! Find a career where you can work remotely from anywhere.

Jobspresso

https://jobspresso.co/

Work remotely from anywhere. Expertly curated online tech, marketing, customer support jobs, and more.

StartUpJobs

https://startupjobs.asia/

Take control of your hiring; register with Startup Jobs Asia today and start posting your roles. Browse exciting jobs from emerging Startups from Asia or, even better, deposit your resume to let Startups look for you.

Working Nomads

https://www.workingnomads.com/jobs

Working Nomads Post a Job Job Alerts. Online jobs for Digital Working Nomads. Work remotely from your home or places around the world. We curate the best digital jobs for those looking to start their telecommuting.

JustRemote

https://justremote.co/

Remote Jobs: Design, Marketing, Programming, Writing & More Remote Jobs That Fit Your Life Discover fully and partially online jobs from the greatest online working companies Remote Jobs.

Gun.Io

https://gun.io/

Vetted job opportunities for world-class engineers.

Work with exceptional technology companies on your terms. We help you land and manage a steady online, long-term work stream.

Remotive

https://remotive.com/

Our mission is to help tech professionals go online.

People Per Hour

https://www.peopleperhour.com/

There's never been a better time to take yourself online and start making money from your fine-tuned skills. Work wherever suits you; choose full-time, part-time, or flexi-time.

Krop

https://www.krop.com/

Krop's Design Job Board has been a mainstay of the creative industry for almost 20 years. Global brands and start-ups alike have supercharged their creative departments with Krop. Search Job Board or Employer Site.

Online teaching jobs are becoming increasingly popular as more and more educational institutions and students seek the convenience and flexibility of virtual learning. Online teaching jobs offer a unique opportunity to make a difference in students' lives worldwide while enjoying the benefits of remote work. Online teachers can work from anywhere in the world, allowing for greater work-life balance and the ability to connect with students from diverse backgrounds. Following is a list of resources and websites offering online teaching jobs.

Digino

A good resource on how to teach online.

https://digino.org/teach-online/

Vip Kid

https://www.vipkid.com/

- Requirements: Hiring native-English speaking US/Canadian applicants with a bachelor's degree. Eligibility to work in the U.S. or Canada. And you must pass a background check to get hired.

- Students: Teaching English online to Chinese students (Kindergarten to grade 9).

- Rate: Pays up to $22/hour.

- Commitments: 6-month minimum commitment lets you choose how little or how much you want to work. However, one important thing to remember is that the company operates in Beijing timezone. You must work around their schedule (for example, Beijing is usually 12 hours ahead of New York).

Bling Abc

https://www.blingabc.com/

- Requirements: Hiring native-English speakers with a bachelor's degree.
- Students: Teaching groups of 3 to 15 Chinese children, and all material is provided.
- Rate: Pay between $21-$27 per hour (depending on how many students are in the class) and pay once a month.
- Commitments: 6-month contract, and BlingABC works on a fixed schedule across four semesters. This means you will have the same weekly schedule for an entire semester.

Q Kids

https://teacher.qkids.com/

- Requirements: Hiring native-English speaking US/Canadian applicants who have completed a bachelor's degree and hold a teaching license or ESL certificate (such as TEFL).
- Students: Teaching English online to Chinese students (Kindergarten to grade 6).
- Rate: Average $18/hour.
- Commitments: Qkids teaching contracts are six months, and the opportunity to extend if you have a good evaluation. Teachers must open up at least 12 class spots per week, and those who teach more than 15 are eligible for a bonus!

Itutor Group

https://join.itutorgroup.com

- Requirements: Hiring native-English-speaking applicants with a bachelor's degree. Applicants must have a TESOL or equivalent/willing to obtain certification.
- Students: Teaching English online to Taiwanese children/adults.
- Rate: Pays up to $24/hour.

- Commitments: A minimum commitment of 5 peak hours per week

51 Talk

https://hk.51talk.com/

- Requirements: Hiring applicants from the Philippines with a bachelor's degree and experience teaching young learners. No TEFL is required.
- Students: Teaching English online to Chinese students aged 4 - 12.
- Rate: Average $17/hour.

Commitments: Each class lasts 25 minutes long, and you must work at least 30 peak time hours per month.

English Hunt

http://www.englishuntusa.com/

- Requirements: Hiring applicants from the United States with 48 college credit hours or an ESL certificate.
- Students: Teaching English on the phone to adult students in Korea.
- Rate: Around $20/hour.

Teach Away

https://www.teachaway.com/online-teaching-jobs

- Requirements: Hiring native-English speaking US/Canadian applicants with a bachelor's degree.
- Students: Teaching English online to Chinese students (preschool to grade 6).
- Rate: Pay varies depending on credentials/experience.

Palfish

https://www.ipalfishclass.com

- Requirements: Hiring fluent English speakers with American, British, Canadian, Australian, New Zealand, and Irish/English dialects. You MUST have a valid teaching certification (TEFL/TESOL/CELTA) or teaching license to teach with PalFish.

- Non-native English-speaking teachers are encouraged to apply. PalFish does not have any preference regarding nationality for teaching positions.

- Degree: Not required

- Rate: Average pay rate is approximately $10-$18 per hour. However, popular teachers charge more than $30 per hour.

- Commitment: As a PalFish teacher, you require no time commitment; it is flexible.

Cambly

https://www.cambly.com/english?lang=en

- Requirements: Hiring native English speakers from the USA, Canada, UK, and Australia, as well as some other countries.

- Degree: No college degree and no certification necessary

- Rate: Pays $0.17 per minute ($10.20 per hour), delivering your earnings every Monday via PayPal.

- Commitment: You make your hours—work as little or as much as you want. You can log in online in your free time and take chat calls within minutes.

Whales English

https://www.whalesenglish.com/

- Requirements: Hiring native-English speakers from English-speaking countries with a BA degree or higher. Experience teaching kids (minimum of 1 year). At least one teaching certificate: TESOL, TEFL, CELTA, etc.

- Students: Typically, 2

- Rate: $18-$30 per 50-minute class, plus performance-based bonuses.

- Commitment: 8 hours/week

- Class Length: 50 minutes + 10 minutes of feedback time.

Tutlo

https://hello.tutlo.com/speak-english-fluently/apply-to-tutlo

- Requirements: A native speaker of English from the US, the UK, Ireland, Australia, New Zealand, Canada, and South Africa. Non-native speakers are welcome to apply. Minimum of 6 months of English teaching experience.
- No college degree and no certification are necessary.
- Rate: Average $5 - $1/ hour

Esl Authority

https://eslauthority.com/

Magic Ears

https://t.mmears.com/v2/home/

Open English

https://www.openenglish.com/en/careers/

A college degree or certification is not mandatory

Italki

https://teach.italki.com/application

A college degree or certification is not necessary

Learnlight

http://careers.learnlight.com/careers-2/teaching-positions

Berlitz

https://www.berlitz.com/careers

THE GOLD MINE OF NEW TECHNOLOGIES

New technologies always offer exciting jobs with usually a lot less competition since there are a lot fewer candidates who are aware of those technologies or have relevant knowledge. It is essential to understand that the job offered is not only technical per-se; in those new fields, you will find various jobs, such as marketers, customer supports, managers, etc... You need to first be on the lookout for those new technologies and then be curious enough to learn about them. Not only will you have a lot less competitive candidates for the offered position, but once you secure a job, it will usually pay better than an equivalent job in a more traditional industry.

One of those new industries is the blockchain and cryptocurrency industry. You probably heard or read somewhere about "Bitcoin." It's a new technology, and hundreds of companies are looking for people with an understanding and experience with cryptocurrency. You can get hired as a developer, community manager, customer service, marketing, content writer, translator, etc...

To learn this skill is quite simple; you can get familiar in a few days—study blockchain technology and how it works. And learn the basics of cryptocurrency and how to use a wallet or an exchange. This field is new; hence there is a lack of knowledgeable people. It provides positions in many jobs if you have cryptocurrency skills.

Another upcoming industry is the Artificial Intelligence (A.I.) industry. Do your research and see if it is something you will enjoy working on.

Exercise

"Why did the job seeker read the classifieds upside down? They were looking for a position to turn their life around!"

Identify two to three platforms that might work for the type of position you are looking for. Then study each of them thoroughly to define which offers you the most benefits based on your situation, including the type of job you are looking for, the fees they take, and the number of potential competitor candidates.

SUBMIT IRRESISTIBLE APPLICATIONS

"A well-crafted job application can help you stand out from the crowd and get noticed by potential employers." - Unknown

Most people fail to understand that looking for a job is a selling exercise. Even if you don't want to work in sales, you must recognize that you are essentially selling your own brand. You are the product, and the employer is the buyer. As with any sales pitch, you must highlight your strengths, showcase your unique selling proposition, and demonstrate why you are the best candidate for the job. This means tailoring your application materials (such as your resume and cover letter) to the specific needs and preferences of the employer and using language that emphasizes your accomplishments and value proposition. It's also important to remember that job hunting is a competitive process, and you are competing against other candidates who are likely also marketing their own brands. You must focus on your strengths and unique competencies to stand out and highlight what makes you the best fit for the job. The better you know yourself, the easier it will be to highlight your value proposition. Treating job hunting as a sales exercise and emphasizing your brand will increase your chances of landing the job of your dreams.

While having the required skills and experiences is essential for any job, employers also want to hire interesting, engaging, and enthusiastic people. Therefore, it is crucial to highlight your personality and demonstrate a passion and commitment to your field of expertise in your application materials and your qualifications.

KNOW THEM BETTER THAN THEY DO

'Researching a company is not just about impressing the interviewer; it's about making sure the company is a good fit for you, too.' - Karyn Mullins

Researching the company before applying for a job or interviewing is essential. This will help you understand the organization's goals, products, and culture and show the employer that you are interested and prepared. Nothing will seduce the interviewer better than if they feel like you are already part of the organization because you speak the same language, understand their industry, and talk about the company as if you have been working there for a while.

Start by looking at the company's website, which will provide basic information such as their markets, products, and contact details. However, keep in mind that the website may present a biased view of the company, so it is essential to look for additional sources of information. One way to gain a more comprehensive understanding of the organization is to research its competitors and market. This will give you a sense of the external factors that may impact the company, such as technological changes, customer preferences, or market trends. Read online reviews about the services provided by the company; it will give you insight into how well the company is perceived and feedback on its products and services.

When preparing for the interview, use your gathered information to formulate questions and insights about the company. This will demonstrate your knowledge and interest in the organization and may spark a meaningful conversation with the interviewer. Not getting overwhelmed by the amount of information you collect is important. Please focus on the most relevant and interesting points, and use them when preparing the application. Avoid simply regurgitating facts from the company's website – add your perspective and insights to make your responses more engaging and thoughtful.

OUTSTANDING RESUME

'A good resume is not just a summary of your past experiences, but a reflection of your future potential.' - Fadi Bishara

What is the purpose of a resume? Most people think it is to give an overview of their academic accomplishments, job experiences, and display of skills. And yes, that is one of the goals of the resume, but the most crucial role of a resume is to get you an interview. It is essential to keep this in mind when writing your resume. You will need to have several resumes, each describing the same fact of your life achievement but focusing on different aspects and accomplishments of your experiences.

Many people fail at that step. They don't understand that the resume is there to get an interview. Write your resume so people want to know more about you. Create intrigue in their mind, either from your highlights on your job experiences or even from your extra-professional activities.

If leadership skill is important for the job, it can be shown in previous employment or with your involvement in some school clubs or activities. It can be demonstrated with your extra curriculum activities. Your values, skills, and motivations must be highlighted at every opportunity in your resume. Stress your achievements; more than just list your past employers and job titles.

When writing your resume, cover letter, and application form, highlight your technical skills, traits, and experiences that make you a good fit for the company. Use the information you have gathered through your research to tailor your application to the organization's needs and values and show why you are the right person for the job.

The style of the content of the resume is highly debated. There are many sources of information and sample templates. We suggest you match your style to the one of the company. Your resume should look different if you apply for an accounting or creative job. Either way, nowadays, everyone includes a little bit of design to catch the reader's attention. Many resumes are now written in Canva, not just Word.

Last but not least, you must understand that your resume needs to get past the first 30 seconds after the recruiter has picked it up. You want your professionalism to stand out and not just stand out because you've used bright yellow highlights! Imagine yours is just one of 50 applications received daily. How can you make your resume and cover letter stand out?

Do's of a resume

- Do tailor your resume to the specific job you are applying for. Highlight the skills and experiences most relevant to the position, and use language and formatting that will catch the employer's attention.

- Do include a clear and concise summary of your qualifications at the top of your resume. This will give the employer a quick overview of your skills and experiences and help them decide whether to read further.

- Do list your experiences in reverse chronological order, starting with your most recent job. This will make it easy for the employer to see your progress and accomplishments over time.

- Do include specific examples of your achievements and contributions in each of your previous roles. Use numbers, percentages, and other metrics to demonstrate the impact of your work.

- Do proofread your resume carefully to avoid typos, grammar, and other mistakes. Ask a friend or family member to review it to catch anything you missed.

- Use a standard and readable font such as Arial and use the same font in your cover letter.

- When listing your previous employers, ensure there are no unexplained gaps. Or know it will be an obvious question at the interview.

Don'ts of a resume

- Don't include irrelevant or outdated information on your resume. Keep it focused on the relevant skills and experiences for the job you are applying for.

- Don't use a generic, one-size-fits-all resume for every job you apply for. Take the time to tailor your resume to each specific position to show how your skills and experiences match the employer's needs.

- Don't use a cluttered or difficult-to-read layout for your resume. Use clear headings, white space, and bullet points to make it easy for the employer to scan and understand your qualifications.

- Don't exaggerate or lie about your skills, experiences, or achievements on your resume. Be honest and accurate in your descriptions, and be prepared to back up your claims with examples during the interview.

- Don't forget to include several contact information on your resume. Include your name, email, mobile, address, and other relevant details that will allow the employer to reach you easily.

- Put only your relevant social media links. For example, highlight your LinkedIn profile, but you might not want to include your Facebook profile with all your vacation and meal photos.

Download the free resume samples workbook:
"Sample resumes based on your profession of choice."
Click here: https://divivo.com/e/resume-workbook

GRABBING COVER LETTER

"A well-written cover letter is a key to unlocking the door to your dream job." - Unknown

Put much effort into the cover letter, even if it is not asked for. If no cover letter is requested, use the email you send your resume as a cover letter; if you submit a web application, use the submission form as a cover letter. The cover letter is where you can make a difference; recruiters expect the resume to be quite robotic and a list of experiences and achievements that they don't always relate to. However, they read the cover letter, especially if your resume passed the 30 seconds test. The cover is your opportunity to make a difference, intrigue the recruiter, and show that your values align with the company's values.

Never use a generic cover letter; those will disqualify you rapidly. Be specific in its content by bringing out one or two elements of how you match what they are looking for. It is not just a wrapper for your resume! Use the cover letter as an opportunity to show that you have done thorough research on the company by bringing specific details or even showing how your skills could add value to the company.

We purposely do not provide sample examples of cover letters to ensure yours will be unique. However, here are some of the questions you might want to answer in your cover letter:

- How do your values and philosophy align with those of the organization?

- Why are you a perfect match for the company? What is the one skill/experience/talent you can provide that will make a difference to the company's results?

- Don't write why you are applying for that company in your cover letter. Too many cover letters explain why the candidate wants to work for an outstanding company. Trying to praise the company hence why they want to be part of the organization. The hiring team doesn't care so much about why you wish to be part of their organization but rather why you will be an asset to them should you join their company.

SUBMIT WITH CONFIDENCE

"Your job application is your first impression with potential employers, so make it count." - unknown

When it comes to the application, it's important to remember that it's an entire package you're presenting to potential employers. From the resume, cover letter, and application form, every detail matters and shouldn't be left to chance. Many online job platforms now add questions to the application, defined by the hiring agent or the field corresponding to the position. Those questions are as important as your resume and cover letter.

Read all the instructions in the application form carefully and comply with them. Employers use these forms for a reason; they do not take too kindly to someone too lazy to be bothered to fill them in appropriately. Adopt a positive attitude throughout the form. Stress achievements when you can. The same elements we learn from the cover letter apply throughout the questions asked in the application form.

Following Up

"Following up shows persistence, determination, and a sincere interest in the job." - Katherine Goldstein

This is a step that applicants too often ignore. Many applicants just wait for an answer. Don't! Be proactive, and follow up on your application. That is an opportunity for your to strike a difference. To remind the hiring agent that you are there, show them that you care enough to follow up with each of your applications rather than making a blast submission to hundreds of companies. One thing it does for sure is to show that you are serious regarding the position and show professionalism. Always an appreciated trait! It makes the life of the hiring agent easier, and you will get on their good side.

Imagine your delight when you receive an email inviting you to attend an interview for this fantastic new job! Preparing for your interviews is the purpose of the next chapter.

ACE YOUR INTERVIEWS

"Interviews are not about being the most qualified; they're about being the most memorable." - Unknown

PREPARING FOR SUCCESS

It is essential to thoroughly prepare for an interview, as you do not want to leave anything to chance. You might have a second chance with a date, but you don't have a second chance with an unprepared interview. Consider the time you spend preparing for the interview as an investment in your potential career. It is better to be over-prepared than under-prepared. As soon as you receive an invitation to interview, start preparing by researching the organization and analyzing your skills and experiences. Set aside focused, uninterrupted time to do this. It is rare to succeed in an interview without proper preparation, even if you have a charming personality and quick wit. Remember that an interview is a one-time opportunity to make a good impression and sell yourself. You must be prepared to answer difficult questions and discuss your personal qualities and experiences. It is not the time to be modest or hold back. Remember, the interview is a selling exercise; you sell yourself from the moment you submit your application or resume.

Timing Is Everything

It is essential to show up at the interview on time or even a few minutes early. Showing up too early makes you appear overly eager or unprepared. Showing up late creates a negative impression on the employer and jeopardizes your chances of getting the job.

A good rule of thumb for an in-person interview is to arrive about ten minutes before the scheduled interview time. This will give the employer enough time to prepare and allow you to settle in and compose yourself before the interview begins.

For a virtual interview, being ready and connected five minutes beforehand will suffice. Make sure you have tested your video and microphone. You don't want to spend the first five minutes asking your interviewer if she can hear you; she certainly will not have the same patience as your grandmother.

If the previous interview runs over or the employer is late, remain patient and professional. Don't let your frustration show, and use the extra time to prepare yourself mentally for the interview. Remember, the employer may be impressed by your ability to stay calm and focused under pressure.

What To Wear

Dressing for a job interview is an important consideration. The right outfit can make a good impression on your potential employer, whereas a wrong impression will jeopardize your chance. However, deciding what to wear can be tricky. It's essential to strike a balance between looking professional and being yourself.

You should aim for a more conservative, formal look when interviewing. One rule of thumb is to dress one level up from the position you are applying for. This could include a suit, dress pants, a button-down shirt, or a knee-length skirt and blouse. Avoid casual clothes like jeans, t-shirts, and sneakers.

It's also important to consider the company's culture and dress code. If you know the company has a more relaxed atmosphere, you can get away with a more casual outfit. However, it's always better to be cautious and dress formally for the interview. In terms of accessories, it's best to keep it simple. Avoid large earrings, bold makeup, and excessive perfume or cologne. If you have tattoos or piercings, consider covering them or removing them for the interview. Ultimately, the most important thing is to feel comfortable and confident in your outfit. If you feel good about your appearance, it will show in your demeanor and make a positive impression on your interviewer.

One way to approach dressing for a job interview is to aim for a professional, well-groomed look. This means avoiding casual or overly fashionable clothing and choosing conservative colors and styles. Wearing a scent that is not overpowering can also create a positive impression. By presenting yourself in a polished and put-together manner, you can show potential employers that you take the interview process seriously and can introduce yourself professionally.

Some of the things for female applicants that are to be avoided are:

- too much jewelry
- remove any visible piercings except discreet earrings
- brightly colored clothes or nail polish
- chewed, unsightly nails
- skirts that are too short and clothes that are too tight or revealing
- accessories that are too colorful or floral
- inappropriate shoes
- collarless shirts
- strong perfume

And for guys:

- pale colored suits
- suit, collar, and no tie combo
- rolled up sleeves
- tattoos on display
- overpowering aftershave
- brown shoes with any color suit except dark brown
- always wear a black belt unless you are wearing a brown suit
- white socks with any outfit
- sandals or any open-toed shoe

These all prove that you do not care about the job and are only worried about your attitude, which may not be a great advertisement for someone looking for a colleague who will fit in. Once you've got the job, there will be plenty of time to assess the "real" dress code of the organization.

The point of dressing yourself well is to leave behind an impression of yourself as well-groomed and professional. Nothing does this as much as the clothes you wear, the fragrance you wear, and the colors you wear. With conservative colors and clothes, you are in the safe zone with most people, whereas a daring fashionable look could disqualify you for too much attitude of the wrong kind.

In-Person Interview

When you arrive at the company for the interview, take the opportunity to gather information and make a good impression. Be polite and thank the person who shows you to the waiting area.

While waiting, use your senses to gather information about the company. Listen for announcements or conversations that may provide insights into the organization's operations or goals. Look around the waiting area for signs of the company's culture, such as mission statements, awards, or photos. If trade magazines or other reading materials are available, scan them for references to the company or interesting information that may be useful during the interview.

Be mindful of your posture and behavior while you are waiting. Sit up straight and avoid sprawling or slouching on the furniture. Be polite and friendly to anyone you encounter, as the interview process begins when you enter the building. Being attentive and professional in the waiting area can make a good impression and set the stage for a successful interview.

Virtual Interview

It is essential to prepare for a virtual interview like you would for an in-person interview. This includes researching the organization, reviewing your resume and cover letter, and preparing reference materials to help you answer questions.

Since the interviewer will not be able to see your entire outfit, it is essential to pay attention to the details that will be visible on the video call. Make sure your clothes are clean, ironed, and appropriate for the job. Check your appearance on the screen to ensure you look professional and presentable.

In addition to your appearance, ensuring your technology works correctly is crucial. Secure a stable internet connection, fully charged batteries, and a quiet location with no background noise. Test your microphone and video settings beforehand to assess if they are working correctly, and check your surroundings to ensure they are appropriate for the call. By taking these steps, you increase your chances that the virtual interview goes smoothly and that you make a good impression on the employer.

Understanding The Employers' Perspective

Knowing what employers think and do during interviews will give you an insight into their processes and thoughts. This will help you better prepare for your interview.

Preparation

During the interview, the employer will likely ask questions based on the job description and person specification used to create the shortlist of candidates. It is essential to review these documents carefully and understand the requirements and expectations for the position. This will help you tailor your answers to show how your skills and experiences match the employer's needs.

The interviewer may use open-ended questions that cannot be answered with a simple "yes" or "no" to encourage you to talk and provide more detailed answers. These questions often begin with words like "what," "why," "how," or "when." Be prepared to do most of the talking, as good interviewing practices typically involve the candidate doing 80% of the talking and the interviewer doing 20%. This allows the employer to get to know you better and understand how you might fit into the organization.

Structure of the Interview

A good interviewer will explain the structure and goals of the interview and provide you with some background information about the company and the position. They might also give you an idea of how long the interview will last and allow time in the end for you to ask any questions you may have.

During the interview, the interviewer may fall silent to allow you to think and provide detailed answers to their questions. If you need a moment to think, it is okay to say so and take a few seconds to gather your thoughts. Don't be afraid to use terms such as "let me think about that for a moment" to ensure they know you haven't just gone blank. Remember that the interviewer may be taking notes, so don't be put off by a lack of eye contact.

At the end of the interview, the interviewer may provide information about the next steps in the hiring process and when a decision will be made. If they don't, it is okay to ask. Remember that interviewers are careful not to make verbal offers or promises that could be interpreted as part of your employment contract. They may say they will recommend you for the job or that an offer will be sent in due course.

Conducting Yourself At The Interview

There is a variety of different types of interviews: such as one-to-one, panel, and group interviews. The style of the interviewers will vary, too – some will seem very stern and assertive, while others will be more welcoming and engaging. In every case, though, there are fundamental principles that you should adopt in how you present yourself and behave during the interview.

- When you first enter the room, ensure you have a good posture and make eye contact with everyone.

- As you are introduced to everyone, give a firm (not too firm) handshake. If you are prone to sweaty palms, discreetly wipe them before you shake hands.

- Scan the room layout once only and maintain eye contact with the lead or only the interviewer.

- Look alert and wait to be asked to sit down.

- If you are offered tea or coffee, politely decline. It's only another thing that can go wrong – like spilling it down yourself or knocking it over!

- Three rules of behavior in the interview are professionalism, professionalism, and professionalism! Stay well away from areas of humor that could be considered offensive. That's not to say you can't use humor where appropriate, but remember, it's not a comedy audition.

- You will likely be asked if you found your way to the interview venue easily. Always answer positively, even if it was a nightmare getting there. These people will be so used to getting to those premises that it will jar in their minds if you moan about not being able to find the building. You are trying to build a consistently positive picture in their mind.

- If you are asked about your well-being, e.g., "How are you today?" never, ever answer in the negative! Not even slightly negative such as "Oh, you know" or "So-so." Be positive and enthusiastic – "Very well, thank you. And you?" This is a typical social interaction that oils the wheels a little. Be polite —end of the lecture.

During an interview, you may be asked to discuss your career to date. While having a copy of your resume in front of you can be helpful, it's essential not to simply repeat what's on the document. Instead, expand on your experiences and achievements, emphasizing your notable contributions. However, be careful not to exaggerate your role in an organization's success. If you were part of a team that achieved results, give credit where credit is due.

In terms of body language, avoid sitting too rigidly or slouching in your chair. Additionally, please don't attempt to mirror the interviewer's body language too closely, as it can come across as fake and manipulative. Instead, be yourself and let your interactions with the interviewer guide whether or not you're a good fit for the position.

The Interviews

The interviews are the final step in the hiring process. If you got that far, it means you have all it takes to do the job; now the remaining question is: "Are you the right fit for the position?". When you are young in your career, the interviews will be focused on your personality and attitude. If you are senior and experienced, the interviews are much more specific and will be more thorough in all aspects, including previous experiences and personality. In most cases, there are several interviews, usually two, although you might have up to four in some cases. The more interviews you go through, the higher your chance of getting hired.

The first interview is for pre-qualification and is meant to check the consistency of your resume. It is a critical interview because you are talking to the gatekeeper. If you succeed in your first interview, your chance of getting the job increase dramatically. The interviewer might be a professional recruiter, so you must prepare well. On the other hand, they might be asking more standard questions. Good preparation will make a big difference.

The longer the interview lasts, the more casual it is and the more chance you have to get the job. A short interview is a tale-tale of a failed interview. It is not a good sign if the interviewer is not enticed or curious about your accomplishments. In that case, you need to turn things around quickly. It could be simply because there is no "chemistry" between you and the interviewer; if you are talking to a Human Resource person, you must realize that this is not the person you will work with. So do your best, stimulate curiosity, ignores the lack of "chemistry," and show your skills and achievements.

It is up to you to make the interview more relaxed and casual. The friendlier the conversation, the more chance you have that the interviewer enjoys the conversation and wants to work with you or have you as part of the team. If the interviewer is a professional recruiter, they will be used to doing interviews; however, if it is your potential manager, they might have less experience or not enjoy interviewing. In that situation, all your communication skills can play a role in making the atmosphere much more relaxed.

The last few interviews are usually done with the person who will supervise you. Your interviewer wants to make sure you will be able to do the job. It might be more focused on your skills and ability. However, even though the interview might be more focused on technical skills and abilities, don't lose track of that personality played a huge role in that second interview. Your potential supervisor needs to feel a connection with you; she needs to want to work with you.

At the end of the interview, when it is your turn to ask questions, your last question should be to ask what is the next step. You may have to be content with the response: "Well, we have a few other candidates to talk to yet, but we will be in touch," At the very least, you can ask, "When am I likely to hear from you?".

Once the interview is finished, always send a thank you note and highlight that you enjoy learning more about the company and the team. Most of the time, this step is ignored and yet significant to show your professionalism and interest in the position.

Take Control

Remember, the interview is not just about the company deciding if you're a good fit for them, but also about you deciding if the company is a good fit for you." - Unknown

It is essential to prepare some questions to ask during the interview. This shows that you are interested in the job and the company and are resourceful enough to come up with thoughtful questions. However, it is also important not to ask too many questions, as this may make the interviewer uneasy or give the impression that you are demanding. Aim to prepare 2-3 questions, and ensure they are your best questions.

The types of questions you ask will depend on where you are in the recruitment process. For example, asking about remuneration or benefits would be inappropriate during an initial stage interview. As you progress through the process, you can ask more detailed and specific questions about the job and the company. By being aware of your questions' appropriate timing and content, you make a good impression on the interviewer and gain valuable information about the job and the organization.

First-Round Interview

During the initial interview, your inquiries should be focused on the nature of the employer's operations and the position you are applying for. For example, an excellent question to ask could be:

"Your company made an operating profit of $Xm last year. Can you share with me any projections for this operating year?"

This question shows that you have researched the company and are interested in its financial performance and prospects. Asking about the company's financial projections can give you valuable insight into the overall health and stability of the organization and help you make an informed decision about whether or not to accept a job offer. Using the word "share" shows that you understand that this information may be sensitive and gives the interviewer an out if they cannot disclose it.

"What opportunities are there for professional development and training within the company?"

Asking about the company's approach to employee development can give you valuable insight into their commitment to supporting the growth and advancement of their staff. This is especially important for professional organizations that require members to demonstrate continuing professional development (CPD) to maintain their membership and credentials. A company that does not provide opportunities for professional development may not be a good fit for your long-term career goals. By asking this question, you can gauge the interviewer's response and determine whether or not the company is committed to supporting the professional growth of its employees. You can also turn the question back on the interviewer by asking them about specific opportunities for training and development within the company.

Asking questions about your potential career trajectory and growth within the company can help you understand the organization's expectations for your performance and potential for advancement. Questions such as *"Where would you see me in five years?"* and *"Has this role been included in any succession planning?"* can give you valuable insight into the company's plans for your development and future within the organization. This can help you determine whether or not the job is a good fit for your long-term career goals and aspirations. Additionally, asking these types of questions can help you identify potential issues with performance management and communication within the company.

Asking about the reporting lines within the organization can help you understand the hierarchy and structure of the company. This is important for understanding the chain of command and whom you will report. It can also help you identify potential career advancement opportunities and understand the company's culture and management style. By asking about the reporting lines, you can gain valuable insight into the organization and determine if it fits your career goals and aspirations well.

Finally, question about performance and expectation.

"What would outstanding performance in this role look like?"

Once they have answered this question, you will at least know how high you have to aim for!

Final-Stage Interview

If you've made it to the second round of interviews, congratulations! This means the company is interested in you and wants to learn more about your skills and experience. To make the most of this opportunity, it's important to continue researching the company, its business, and its market. By understanding these factors, you'll be able to ask informed questions and show off your knowledge during the interview. Additionally, this is a great chance to learn more about working for the company and understand its culture. By asking the right questions and showing interest and enthusiasm, you can impress the interviewer and increase your chances of getting the job.

Now is the moment for you to ask them questions that will both show them that you understand what was mentioned to you during the initial interview, as well as questions that will elicit replies from them that will help you decide whether or not you want to work for them.

Some sample questions:

"You mentioned when we first met that the company was expanding into Asia. What does this mean for the US operation?"

"You said at our initial discussion that additional mechanization of your business was not planned. Can this lack of mechanization be a long-term strategy, or is it prone to change given that most American companies cannot compete with Chinese manufacturers on pricing due to their cheap labor costs?"

"Why do people enjoy working in your firm?"

"What were the key findings of your most recent staff survey?"

"What words would you use to define the atmosphere and culture of this organization?"

"What is your employee turnover level?"

THE RIGHT WAY TO HANDLE QUESTIONS

"The key to a successful job interview is preparation, practice, and confidence." - Unknown

Your interview preparation might make the difference between getting the job and not. You want to be ready to answer any question; the last thing you want is to be speechless on tricky questions. That would show your lack of preparation and knowledge and simply the fact that you are not resourceful, precisely the opposite of what a recruiter is looking for. So many people are anxious when they get an interview. The truth is, it is a pretty straightforward exercise when you are ready for any question. Knowing your answers to the most commonly asked questions will allow you to focus more on the delivery and your presentation during the interviews rather than digging into your subconscious to find an answer. That is the purpose of this chapter.

All questions are organized by sections. You must know how to answer at least the basic interview questions. Salary and career development questions are classic and will probably be asked as well. Then there are different sections for different competencies and skills. Review the questions related to the requirements for the position you are applying for. The last few sections are optional, but it can only help you to review those questions.

We provided sample answers for quite a lot of questions. We can't give you a sample answer for a question such as "Tell me about yourself." While reading the possible answers to the interview questions, don't focus so much on the answer itself but more on how we answer the questions. Each time a question is asked, you must highlight your successes, positive contributions to the organization or the team, and competencies you have mastered and are required for the position you apply to.

This chapter should be a great help so you are not caught off guard during the interviews by difficult questions but instead dazzle the interviewers with your confidence and clarity in answering all their questions. Pay attention to all sample answers. They also give you insights into what employers seek regarding personality, attitude, and presence. You will not get a job if you fail the interview. Understand the stakes, and prepare yourself accordingly.

For your convenience, all the questions are sorted and organized by competencies.

Basic Interview Questions

Tell me about yourself.

Why did you apply for this job?

What are some of your strengths?

What are a few of your weaknesses?

In your opinion, what is the ideal company?

What makes you want to work for this company?

Where would you like to be in your career five years from now?

Why should we hire you?

What did you like least about your last job?

When were you most satisfied with your job?

Tell me about the responsibilities you held in your last job.

Why are you leaving your present job?

What do you know about this industry?

What do you know about our company?

Are you willing to relocate?

What makes you the best candidate for this job?

Do you have any questions for me?

Salary Questions

What have you made as a salary in the past?

What salary are you seeking?

If we were to offer you the salary you requested, but you had to write your job description for the first year of employment, what would it say?

Career Development Questions

What are you looking for in terms of career development?

How do you want to improve yourself in the next year?

What goals would you have in mind if you got this job?

If your previous supervisor were to recommend any additional exposure or training for you, what would they suggest?

Critical Thinking Questions

Questions like this are used in various contexts, regardless of the level of position you are applying for. Regardless of your natural talent, the interviewer is interested in your decision-making process. It is essential to note that different situations require different decision-making processes. Although it would be ideal for gathering all the facts and weighing them up, sometimes you may have to make decisions based on incomplete information or gut instinct. However, it is crucial to show how you react to the situation and learn from the outcome. Sharing an experience where the outcome was unfavorable, but you learned a valuable lesson, can demonstrate your resilience and ability to progress to the interviewer.

Q: Tell us about a recent situation in which you had to decide without having all the facts.

A: In my previous job, I was tasked with deciding whether to pursue a potential new client, but unfortunately, the information we had about their budget and specific needs was incomplete. I had to weigh the pros and cons of pursuing this potential opportunity without all the information we would typically have.

To make an informed decision, I consulted with colleagues who had experience working with similar clients and researched the industry to get a better sense of typical budgets and requirements. I also reached out to the potential client to ask more specific questions about their needs and budget, but unfortunately, they could not provide much more information at the time.

Based on my limited information, I decided to pursue the opportunity. Although it was a bit of a risk, we had a strong track record with similar clients, and we could offer them a valuable service that would meet their needs.

In the end, the decision paid off, and we were able to win the new client's business. However, I also learned the importance of gathering as much information as possible before making a decision, as it can help mitigate risks and increase the chances of success.

Q: How do you usually go about solving a problem?

A: When faced with a problem, I typically follow a four-step process. Firstly, I gather all the relevant information on the issue. This could involve consulting colleagues or researching online. Secondly, I analyze the data to identify the root cause of the problem. Once I have identified the root cause, I brainstorm potential solutions. Lastly, I evaluate the possible solutions and select the most effective and feasible ones.

Of course, the specifics of the process can vary depending on the problem and context. For example, some issues may require extensive research or consulting with multiple stakeholders. Regardless of the situation, I always strive to approach problems in a methodical and structured manner to ensure that I am addressing the root cause and selecting the best possible solution.

Q: Would you say you are good at making decisions?

A: Yes, I am good at making decisions. I approach decision-making by gathering all the available information, weighing the pros and cons of each option, and considering the potential outcomes and consequences. I also think about any potential risks and anticipate any challenges that may arise. Once I have all of this information, I make a decision that is in the organization's and its stakeholders' best interest. I also regularly evaluate the results of my decisions and make adjustments as needed.

Q: In what past situations have you shown sound judgment? What did you do precisely that was effective?

A: I have shown sound judgment in a variety of past situations. For example, when working in a restaurant, I dealt with a customer causing a disturbance and making other customers uncomfortable. I calmly approached the customer and politely asked them to lower their voice and stop causing a disruption. When they refused, I decided to call the manager and have them handle the situation. This decision was right because it ensured the other customers' safety and comfort and protected the restaurant from legal issues.

In another situation, I was working on a team project, and we had to decide which approach to take. I carefully considered the pros and cons of each option and made a recommendation based on my analysis. My teammates agreed with my recommendation, and we completed the project on time and to our client's satisfaction.

I have demonstrated sound judgment in various situations by being thoughtful, objective, and decisive.

Q: Think of someone with excellent judgment – what do they do exactly?

A: Someone who shows excellent judgment can assess a situation quickly and accurately and make a decision that is in the best interests of the people involved and the situation at hand. They can think critically and objectively and consider the potential consequences of their actions. They are also able to act confidently and decisively without hesitation or uncertainty.

Q: Describe the last time you had to make a spur-of-the-moment decision. Why was this necessary? How did your decision affect others? What consequences had you not considered?

A: The last time I had to make a spur-of-the-moment decision was when I was driving and came to an intersection where the traffic lights were out. I had to assess the situation and decide what to do quickly. I looked carefully to see if there were any other vehicles or pedestrians and then decided to proceed through the intersection cautiously. I was able to navigate the intersection and continue on my way safely.

Overall, good judgment involves being aware of the situation, thinking critically, and acting decisively.

Q: Tell us when you took responsibility for making a critical decision. What was your conclusion? How did you defend your decision? What was the possible impact of a poor decision?

A: I have taken responsibility for making a critical decisions on several occasions. For example, when I was working as a team leader on a project, we had to decide which approach to take to meet the project deadline. The other team members were unsure of which direction to go, so I took the lead and made a recommendation based on my analysis of the situation. I presented my proposal to the team and explained its reasons, and they agreed with my decision. We successfully completed the project on time and to our client's satisfaction.

Another time, I had to decide how to handle a difficult customer making unreasonable demands. I listened to the customer's concerns and tried to resolve the issue, but they were not satisfied with my response. I realized the situation would not be fixed to the customer's satisfaction, so I escalated the issue to my manager. My manager handled the situation more effectively, and the customer eventually calmed down and accepted the resolution.

Overall, I have demonstrated the ability to take responsibility for making critical decisions and to do so thoughtfully and decisively.

Q: Describe a time when you referred a decision upwards. What was the background? Why did you need help? To what extent do you seek advice?

A: I have referred to a decision upward several times, but one situation stands out. I was working in a customer service role and received a call from a customer who was extremely upset about a billing error. I tried to resolve the issue, but the customer was not satisfied with my response and continued to escalate the situation. I realized the customer would not be happy with any resolution I could offer, so I escalated the issue to my manager. My manager was able to handle the situation more effectively and was able to provide the customer with the information and resolution they were looking for.

Referring to the decision upward was right in this situation because it ensured that someone with the authority and expertise addressed the customer's concerns. It also allowed me to focus on my other responsibilities and avoid getting bogged down in a situation that would not be resolved to the customer's satisfaction.

Overall, referring a decision upwards is appropriate when the situation is beyond my authority or expertise or when it will not be resolved to the satisfaction of the customer or other stakeholders.

Q: Tell us about a recent situation in which you had to be objective when deciding. What were the facts you had to review? How did you weigh the different pieces of information? Looking back, what do you think of your decision?

A: Recently, I had to be objective when deciding on a problem that arose at work. I was working on a team project, and one of my teammates made a mistake that had significant consequences. The error could have jeopardized the project's *success, and the other team members were upset and angry. I had to decide how to address the situation and move forward.*

I took the time to assess the situation objectively without letting my emotions or personal biases influence my decision. I looked at the facts and considered the potential consequences of different actions. I also consulted with my manager and other relevant stakeholders to gather their input and advice. Based on this objective analysis, I decided to have the mistake corrected and put measures in place to prevent it from happening again. I also decided to have a team meeting to discuss the issue and develop a plan to move forward.

Overall, I made a fair and objective decision that addressed the mistake and its consequences and ensured that the project could continue and be completed successfully. Being objective is essential when making decisions because it allows me to consider all relevant information and perspectives and decide in the best interests of the situation and the people involved.

Q: How would you describe your preferred style of making judgments? What are the key strengths of this? How does this compare with your colleagues" style?

A: My preferred judgment style is to be thoughtful, objective, and decisive. It is essential to carefully consider all relevant information and perspectives when making a decision and to avoid letting my emotions, or personal biases influence my judgment. I also try to be open-minded and consider alternative viewpoints, even if they differ.

When deciding, I take the time to assess the situation and gather input from relevant stakeholders. I also consider the potential consequences of different actions and weigh each option's pros and cons before deciding. Once I have made a decision, I communicate it clearly and confidently, and I am willing to defend my decision if necessary.

Overall, my preferred judgment style is effective because it allows me to make fair and objective decisions that are in the best interests of the situation and the people involved.

Q: How would you describe your preferred style of making decisions? Where do you typically source your information?

A: My preferred decision-making style is to be thoughtful, objective, and decisive. It is essential to carefully consider all relevant information and perspectives when making a decision and to avoid letting my emotions, or personal biases influence my judgment. I also try to be open-minded and consider alternative viewpoints, even if they differ.

When deciding, I take the time to assess the situation and gather input from relevant stakeholders. I also consider the potential consequences of different actions and weigh each option's pros and cons before deciding. Once I have made a decision, I communicate it clearly and confidently, and I am willing to defend my decision if necessary.

Overall, my preferred decision-making style is effective because it allows me to make fair and objective decisions that are in the best interests of the situation and the people involved.

Q: We all have to make unpopular decisions that may affect others. Describe a situation when you have had to make such a decision. Why did you take it? How did the people who were affected react? What did you learn from this experience?

A: I have had to make unpopular decisions that may affect others several times. For example, when I was working as a manager in a retail store, I had to decide to lay off some of the employees due to budget cuts. This was a difficult decision because I knew that it would affect the employees who were losing their jobs, and it would also impact the overall productivity and morale of the team.

However, I knew the budget cuts were necessary to keep the store financially viable and protect the remaining employees' jobs. I decided to lay off the employees and explained the situation to them and the rest of the team. I also supported and assisted the affected employees and addressed concerns or issues.

Making unpopular decisions is sometimes necessary to achieve the best outcome for the situation and the people involved. I make these decisions carefully and with consideration for the impact they may have on others.

Q: Can you tell us when you had to source information from various sources and make business judgments based on it? Talk us through the actual steps you took in this process.

A: I have had to source information from various sources and make business judgments based on it several times. For example, when I was working as a market research analyst, I had to gather and analyze data from multiple sources to make recommendations to my clients. This involved collecting data from surveys, focus groups, market reports, and industry publications and synthesizing the information to identify trends and patterns.

Based on this information, I had to judge market conditions, consumer behavior, and competitor strategies to provide my clients with insights and recommendations. I had to carefully consider the information's accuracy and reliability and verify it with multiple sources to make accurate and reliable judgments.

Overall, being able to source information from various sources and make business judgments is crucial for anyone in a business or market research role. It requires critical thinking, attention to detail, and synthesizing complex information.

Strategic Thinking Questions

If you feel this section is not for you because you have never held a position requiring you to think "strategically," resist the urge to skip it. There are other aspects of strategy besides high-level corporate decision-making. It involves planning past the completion of the current task. You probably do it frequently, but don't call it "strategy" or anything else so lofty.

After reading a few examples, consider instances where you have looked past the tip of your nose. It might have been as simple as organizing your diary or engaging in the "long game" of office politics.

Q: In what past situations have you shown the most evidence of visionary/strategic thinking?

Respond by describing a time when you could see things from a different angle. The key here is to avoid getting bogged down in unnecessary detail, which will eventually bore your interviewers. They won't share your frame of reference and won't be able to be familiar with the relevant characters. They should be succinct but provide enough information to convey the main points, just like your other interview responses.

A: One situation that comes to mind is when I worked for XYZ Company as a marketing manager. We were facing increased competition from new players in the market, and our sales were declining. We needed a more strategic approach to our marketing efforts to stay competitive and grow our market share.

I conducted a thorough analysis of our target audience and the market trends. Then I developed a comprehensive marketing strategy that involved revamping our branding, optimizing our digital channels, and launching a targeted campaign that focused on the unique value proposition of our products. I also worked closely with the sales team to align our efforts and ensure we met our goals.

As a result, we increased our market share by 15% within six months, and our sales started to trend upward again. This experience taught me the importance of strategic thinking and its impact on a company's success. My ability to think strategically, analyze data, and develop effective plans can add value to any organization I work for.

Q: What do you see as the main threats to our business in the long term? What can we do to ensure long-term success?

Most employers will anticipate that you have done some online research on them. This strategy will provide you with a wealth of data and facts about them that they want you to know. A company's website won't provide details about its rivals, the market state, or any developments that its competitors may have that could affect its position in the market. Then, when conducting your research, find out who their direct rivals are and visit their websites. Consider acquiring a global perspective of their market. Consider what outside factors may have an impact on their goods or services. The introduction of smoke-free workplaces, for instance, may have had a negative impact on businesses that produce smoking-related goods like tobacco, paper, filters, etc., but a positive impact on companies that provide employers with "no smoking" signs or make smoking shelters, for instance.

A: Based on my research and understanding of your industry, the main threats to your business in the long term are increasing competition and rapid technological changes. As the market grows, more companies will likely enter and compete for market share. Staying ahead of the curve and continually innovating to maintain your competitive edge is essential. Additionally, emerging technologies could disrupt your current business model, so staying up-to-date and adapting to changing market conditions is essential. It's critical to proactively identify and address these threats through investing in research and development, strategic partnerships, or other means.

Q: Tell me about a recent time you took a broad view of your work. Why was this necessary? How useful was this approach?

A: Recently, I took a broad view of my work while trying to improve my efficiency and productivity. I realized that I had been getting bogged down in the details of my tasks and wasn't making as much progress as I wanted. So, I took a step back and looked at the big picture of my work. I evaluated my goals and priorities and identified the areas where I could make the most significant impact. I also assessed my strengths and weaknesses and devised a plan to focus on the tasks I was best suited to do. As a result, I worked more efficiently and effectively and made significant progress on my projects.

Q: How do you think the role for which you are applying will impact the long-term success of the company? How do you see your contribution? What do you know of this company's long-term strategy?

A: The role I am applying for will impact the company's long-term success by bringing new skills and perspectives to the team. As someone with experience in [relevant field or skill], I can bring a fresh perspective and a deep understanding of the latest trends and developments in the industry. I am also a strong collaborator and communicator and am committed to working closely with my team members to achieve our shared goals. These qualities will enable me to contribute positively to the company's long-term success and growth.

Q: Give an example of a time when you could have taken a more long-term view of a project/strategy. Why was this important? What was the outcome? What did you learn?

A: One time I could have taken a more long-term view of a project was when working on a marketing campaign for a new product. I was focused on delivering immediate results and was eager to see the campaign perform well in the short term. However, I should have considered how the campaign would impact the company's long-term goals and objectives. In hindsight, I should have taken a broader, more strategic view of the campaign and looked at how it would fit into the overall plan for the product. Taking a long-term perspective, I could have made more informed decisions and contributed to the company's overall success.

Drive For Achievement Questions

Q: Tell me what you know about our business.

Just repeating facts from a website won't make you stand out. Digging deeper and understanding the company beyond the surface level is important. Find out their market share, competitors, threats to their growth, and potential opportunities to capitalize on. Don't just rely on the information presented to you by the company, but also research their competitors and reach out to their marketing department for their most recent annual report.

The internet is helpful, but going beyond the obvious information is essential. Imagine interviewing multiple candidates who all repeat the same information they found online. But what if one candidate mentions that the company is currently second in the world market, but the CEO has a strategy to take them to number one? This would make them stand out and earn them a final interview.

Therefore, it's crucial to be creative and think outside the box when demonstrating your knowledge about a company during an interview.

Q: Give an example of when you've experienced a setback.

If this question is asked to you at an interview and you are unprepared, you may mess it up without a doubt. The interviewer is mining a negative vein, and your default response will be to deny it. After all, someone as smart as I always get things right on the first try, right?

The key is to think back to a situation in which, despite a successful ending, you were responsible for it through either your intervention or your recognition that what you did the first time was ineffective. There is no shame in acknowledging that your original approach to a scenario wasn't as successful as you'd wanted. Still, because of your strong self-awareness, you could adjust some or all components and ultimately succeed in your goal.

Interviewers will want you to describe the circumstance, your reasoning for doing what you first did, how you reacted after realizing it wasn't working, and maybe how those around you reacted. For instance:

A: One example of a setback I experienced was when I was working on a project for a client. Initially, I approached the project with a specific strategy in mind, but as I worked on it, I realized that this approach would not be effective. Instead of continuing this approach, I took a step back and reassessed the situation. Through my self-awareness and problem-solving skills, I developed a new strategy and successfully completed the project.

My initial approach did not produce the desired results, but I overcame this setback by recognizing the problem and adapting my approach. This experience taught me the importance of adaptability and flexibility in facing challenges.

This response includes all the necessary components, including a description of the situation, your initial strategy, your realization that it wasn't working, the development of a new solution and its success, and finally, an admission of your original error.

Q: What have you done to progress your education to date?

Regarding formal schooling, I cannot tell you what to say because you will all have different experiences. Yet education may take many other forms. Therefore you should discuss this with excitement...

A: To date, I have progressed my education through various means. Regarding formal education, I have completed a bachelor's degree in [Subject] and am currently enrolled in a master's program in [Subject]. I have also taken several courses and workshops to expand my knowledge and skills in specific areas, such as [Course/Workshop].

Additionally, I am an avid learner, always looking for opportunities to learn new things. I am also continuously self-study, reading books and articles related to my field to deepen my knowledge and understanding. I regularly attend conferences and seminars to stay up-to-date on the latest developments in my field. I am also an active member of professional organizations that provide educational resources and networking opportunities.

As an enthusiastic and loyal employee, I always seek ways to improve and expand my skill set. I recognize the importance of obtaining industry-specific formal qualifications, and I am committed to continuing my education to stay at the forefront of my field. Additionally, I am proactive in my career and always seek new opportunities to learn and grow. These qualities make me an asset to any employer.

From the employer's perspective, this response communicates several desirable traits, including zeal, loyalty, a desire to advance your career, a willingness to broaden your skill set, a recognition of the value of industry-specific formal qualifications, and a willingness to expand your skill set.

Q: Do you think you are overqualified?

Why on earth would you be asked this question during an interview? Before they chose to interview you, didn't they read your resume? You may be sure that they are not concerned about this since if they were, they would have rejected you during the initial sift. They're attempting to determine whether or not they were fortunate enough to get a Lamborghini for the price of a Mercedes. Turn the tables on them.

A: If you are concerned that I may be overqualified for this position, I am dedicated and committed to any project I undertake. I have a strong work ethic and do not get bored quickly. Instead, I thrive in challenging and dynamic environments and always look for ways to learn and grow. I am confident in my abilities and can do an excellent job in this role.

While I am certainly open to the possibility of advancement within the organization in the future, my immediate goal is to do the best job possible in the position I am being considered for. Furthermore, I am excited about the opportunity to join your team and contribute to the company's success. I am eager to discuss this further and address any concerns you may have.

Q: Do you mind reporting to someone younger than you?

A: I have no problem working with and reporting to someone younger than me. Competency and experience are the most important factors in leadership and job performance. If someone has proven themselves competent and worthy of their position, I have no issue with working with them, regardless of their age.

Furthermore, I always strive to improve and excel in my work, to become a valuable and respected team member. I am willing to learn from those with more experience and expertise, and I am open to one day being in a position where I am responsible for leading and mentoring others.

Q: Which is more important to you, the job or your salary?

I bet you now believe they are attempting to get you to accept that you are selfish and money-driven, right? You realize that interviewers are realistic. Although polls show that money isn't usually the most crucial aspect of a job, only some of us would work for nothing! Mentioning pay in your response is okay.

A: It is essential to consider both the job and the salary when deciding on a career or job opportunity. While a high salary can motivate, it is not the only factor I consider. The job itself, including the work environment, the company culture, and the potential for growth and advancement, are also important considerations to me. Ultimately, finding a fulfilling, challenging job that aligns with my career goals and values is the most critical factor.

Q: Why should we employ you rather than one of the other candidates?

You didn't anticipate that one, did you? Should you cast aspersions on the other candidates to make yourself look better? Obviously not! Just how could you be? What distinguishing trait makes you the ideal candidate? asks the interviewer.

You must demonstrate that you have researched the company and the job description to stand out. You should be prepared to show how your abilities, credentials, and successes meet the employer's needs. It's crucial to come across as genuinely excited about the job.

A: I am the best candidate for this position because I have the skills, experience, and passion required for the job. I have a strong track record of success in similar roles, and I am confident in my ability to hit the ground running and positively contribute to the team. Additionally, I am highly motivated, dedicated, and committed to putting in the time and effort necessary to excel in this position.

I have excellent communication skills and can effectively collaborate with colleagues and clients. I am also highly adaptable and can quickly learn new skills and processes. Furthermore, I am a team player and can work well with others to achieve common goals.

In short, I am the best candidate for this position because I have the necessary skills, experience, and dedication to succeed. I am confident that I can contribute to the team and the company.

Q: In your job, what is "good enough"?

This is a chance for you to highlight both your commitment to quality and your work ethic.

A: Regarding my work, I don't believe in settling for "good enough." I strive to deliver high-quality work that meets or exceeds expectations consistently. I understand that there may be limitations on time or resources, but I always aim to go above and beyond to produce work that I am proud of, which adds value to the organization. At the same time, I also recognize the importance of balancing perfectionism with efficiency and productivity to ensure that projects are completed on time and within budget.

Q: Tell us about a time when you have been incredibly motivated. What most strongly motivates you to work hard? How does this show itself?

A: One time I was especially motivated was when I was working on a project for a client facing a tight deadline. The client depended on me to deliver the project on time and to their specifications, and I was determined to exceed their expectations. I worked long hours and put in extra effort to ensure the project was completed on time and to the highest possible standard.

Throughout the project, I was highly motivated and focused on achieving the best possible outcome. I was energized by the challenge and the opportunity to demonstrate my skills and capabilities. This experience was incredibly motivating and reinforced my belief in my ability to succeed in challenging situations. Ultimately, the client was delighted with the final product, and I exceeded their expectations.

Q: Tell us about a time when you worked especially hard. Which aspects of the situation motivated you to work hard? Which part of the situation demotivated you? What feedback did you receive on your performance?

A: One time when I worked especially hard was when I was leading a team on a complex and time-sensitive project. The project involved a lot of coordination and collaboration among team members, and I was responsible for ensuring that everyone was on track and working effectively together.

I was determined to see the project through to completion and committed to delivering the best possible results. To achieve this, I worked long hours and put in extra effort to guide and support my team members. I also regularly communicated with the client to inform them of our progress and address any concerns or issues.

Ultimately, the project was successful, and we delivered it on time and within budget. This was a challenging and demanding experience, but I was proud of the hard work and dedication my team, and I put into the project. It was a rewarding experience, reinforcing my belief in the importance of hard work and determination to succeed.

Q: Describe a recent opportunity when you had to take on new responsibilities. How did the opportunity arise? What were these new responsibilities? What was the outcome?

A: A recent opportunity when I had to take on new responsibilities was when I was asked to lead a team on a high-profile project for a key client. This was a significant opportunity for me, as it was a complex and challenging project that required me to take on a leadership role. I was excited about the opportunity but felt pressure and responsibility to deliver successful results.

I was responsible for coordinating the team's work and ensuring we were on track to meet the project's deadlines and objectives. To take on these new responsibilities, I had to quickly learn about the project and its goals, as well as the skills and capabilities of my team members. I also had to establish clear goals and expectations for the team and provide guidance and support as needed.

Ultimately, the project succeeded, and I demonstrated my leadership skills and capabilities. This experience was challenging and demanding, but it was also gratifying. It allowed me to take on new responsibilities and grow as a professional.

Q: Give an example of when you set an ambitious target. What made it so ambitious? How did it compare with other targets you had set yourself? How well did you do?

A: One time I set myself an ambitious target was when I decided to run a marathon. I had never run more than a few miles at a time before, and the thought of running 40 kilometers seemed impossible to me. But I was determined to challenge myself and see what I could do. I trained hard for several months, gradually increasing my distance and speed. On race day, I set a pace that I thought was realistic and pushed myself to keep going, even when it felt difficult. In the end, I was able to finish the marathon and achieve my ambitious target. It was a proud moment, and I learned much about my determination and resilience.

Q: Describe a situation in which you had to work under pressure. What was the cause of the stress? How did you feel under this pressure? What impact did this have on your work?

A: One situation in which I had to work under pressure was when I was leading a team to meet a tight deadline for a project. We had to complete a major software update for one of our clients, and the deadline was only a few days away. We had to overcome many challenges and obstacles, and sometimes it felt like the project would fail. But I kept everyone focused and motivated, and we were able to work efficiently and effectively to get the update finished on time. It was challenging and stressful, but I rose to the occasion and led my team to success.

Q: Tell me about a crisis you have handled recently. What caused it? What did you do to resolve it? What were your feelings at the time?

A: Recently, I had to handle a crisis at work when one of our key suppliers failed to deliver a crucial component on time. This put our entire production schedule at risk and could have resulted in significant delays and financial losses for the company. I quickly organized a team to assess the situation and identify alternative suppliers who could provide the necessary component. We secured the component from another supplier and delivered it in time to meet our production schedule. Although it was a stressful situation, I was able to stay calm and focused, and I was able to successfully lead my team through the crisis and prevent any significant disruptions.

Q: Tell us about a time when you felt unfairly criticized. Why was this? How did you respond? What was the outcome?

A: I felt unfairly criticized while working on a group project at school. I was in charge of a particular part of the project and put much effort into it. But when we presented the project to the class, one of my classmates criticized my work and pointed out everything wrong. Their criticism was unfair because they didn't understand the context or constraints I was working under and didn't take the time to appreciate the effort I had put into my part of the project. It was a frustrating and hurtful experience, but I learned from it, and I try to be more understanding and supportive of others in similar situations.

Q: Describe a situation at work when something was causing you to feel negative. What caused these feelings? How did you approach your work at the time? What impact did this have on your colleagues?

A: One situation at work when I was feeling negative was when I was assigned to a project with a difficult team member. This person was always pessimistic, and they tended to blame others for any problems or challenges that came up. It was hard to stay positive and motivated when working with this person, and I dreaded our meetings and interactions. I tried to remain professional and focused on the project, but it was challenging to maintain a positive attitude in the face of their negativity. Eventually, I talked to my manager about the situation, and we came up with a solution that made the project more manageable and enjoyable for everyone involved.

Q: Can you tell us when your drive and determination inspired others to commit more to their work? What was the result? What did you say? How did other people respond?

A: I led a team on a significant project when my drive and determination inspired others to commit more to their work. The project was complex and challenging, requiring everyone to put in much effort and dedication. I was very passionate about the project and determined to see it through to success, no matter what obstacles we faced. I clearly communicated my vision and goals to the team and set a high standard for excellence and hard work. As the project progressed, I saw my enthusiasm and determination inspired others to give their best effort and be more committed. In the end, we delivered a high-quality product that exceeded our client's expectations, which was a source of pride for the entire team.

Relationship Building Questions

In most work environments, employees are expected to interact with others to some degree. Potential employers seek assurance that you will "fit in" with their team. You may wonder if this is necessary, playing the role of a devil's advocate. However, consider how you would feel if a new person joined your social group.

Would you expect them to fit in with your group's norms, or would you think it's your group's responsibility to adjust to the new person? You should expect the latest person to adapt.

Employers use this approach for two reasons. They want to know if you can build relationships as it's a job requirement, or they want to ensure that you have a personality similar to the team you would be joining. My advice is to be true to yourself. If you pretend to be someone you're not just to fit in and you get the job, your true self will eventually come out, potentially causing conflicts. It's challenging to sustain a persona that doesn't reflect your true self. Furthermore, you may regret the job if you realize that your new colleagues "are not your kind of people" either.

Q: Tell me about a recent situation when you had to build a relationship with a new colleague. Why was the relationship important?

A: In my previous job, I led a cross-functional project team that included a colleague from a different department I had never worked with before. Initially, we had different ideas for approaching the project, creating tension between us. However, I recognized the importance of building a solid relationship with this colleague to ensure the project's success.

I communicated with my colleagues regularly and listened to their concerns and ideas to build a relationship. I also tried to find common ground between our perspectives and worked to find a compromise that addressed our concerns. Through this process, we developed a strong working relationship that allowed us to collaborate effectively and complete the project on time and within budget.

The relationship was meaningful because this colleague had expertise in an area critical to the project's success. By building a solid working relationship, we could leverage each other's strengths and ensure the project met all its objectives. Additionally, the positive working relationship that we developed allowed us to continue collaborating on other projects, which helped to strengthen our department's overall capabilities.

Q: Think of someone who's particularly effective at building and maintaining relationships with others. What do they do exactly?

This question asks not only if you are self-aware but also if you can recognize similar qualities in others. The key here is to use the appropriate adjectives to describe this person, whether real or imaginary.

A: I know a colleague who is exceptional at building and maintaining relationships with others. Her ability to listen actively and empathize with others makes her so compelling. She's genuinely interested in what others say and takes the time to get to know them beyond their professional role. She also makes a point to follow up with people and stay in touch through casual check-ins or sending articles or resources that might be helpful. I've noticed that people appreciate her approach and often come to her for advice or to bounce ideas off. Overall, her success in building relationships comes down to her authenticity, curiosity, and willingness to invest time and energy into others.

Q: How do you behave when you meet new people?

You may act differently every time you meet a new person. However, they wouldn't ask you a question like this and expect a response that basic, would they? Are you self-aware enough of your behaviors and how they affect others, is what they are trying to say here. Can you change depending on the personality or temperament of the person you are with?

A: When I meet new people, I am friendly and approachable. I make eye contact, smile, and introduce myself. I'm interested in getting to know the person, so I ask questions about their background, interests, and experiences. I also find common ground to build a connection. Additionally, it's essential to be respectful and mindful of cultural differences or social norms that may exist. Overall, I am open-minded and non-judgmental and create a positive first impression.

Q: Give me an example of someone coming to you for support or guidance. Why did they need your support? What did you do to support/guide them? How did it help?

A: One time when someone came to me for support and guidance was when I mentored a group of interns at my company. One of the interns, who was new to the industry, was struggling with a project, and they came to me for help. I listened carefully to their concerns and provided guidance and support to help them overcome their challenges. I also advised them on how to approach similar problems in the future and encouraged them to continue learning and growing in their career. I was happy to be able to help them, and I was glad that they felt comfortable coming to me for support.

Q: Describe a time when you had to establish an effective relationship quickly. What did you do? What was the outcome? What did you learn from this?

One time when I had to establish an effective relationship quickly was when I was assigned to a new project at work, and I was working with a team of people whom I had never met before. The project was time-sensitive, and we had to hit the ground running, so I knew it was essential to establish a good working relationship with my teammates as soon as possible. I tried to get to know them and understand their strengths and weaknesses, and I worked hard to communicate openly and honestly with them. I also took the time to listen to their ideas and incorporate their feedback into our plan. By establishing an effective relationship quickly, we could work together effectively and efficiently to complete the project on time.

Q: In what past situations have you been most effective in building and maintaining relationships with others? What did you specifically do that was effective?

A: I have been most effective in building and maintaining relationships where I can communicate openly and honestly, listen to others, and understand their perspectives. For example, I have successfully built and maintained relationships with my coworkers by being a good team player and respecting and considering their ideas and contributions. I have also effectively built and maintained relationships with clients by being responsive and attentive to their needs and transparent and honest in all my interactions with them. My ability to communicate effectively and show genuine interest in others has been critical to building and maintaining relationships.

Q: In which situations have you been least effective in building and maintaining relationships with others? What did you do that detracted from effectiveness? What would you have done differently?

A: I have been least effective in building and maintaining relationships with others in situations where I cannot communicate openly and honestly or where I cannot listen to others and understand their perspectives. For example, I have struggled to build and maintain relationships with coworkers who are very different from me regarding their values, beliefs, and backgrounds. I have also had difficulty building and maintaining relationships with clients who are very demanding or who have unrealistic expectations. In these situations, I have not been able to establish a good rapport or build trust, and as a result, the relationships have not been as effective or productive as I would have liked. I have learned from these experiences and am now more aware of the importance of communication and understanding in building and maintaining relationships with others.

Q: What can you do to become more effective in this competency? What behaviors could you demonstrate more/less?

A: To become more effective in this competency, I plan to focus on improving my communication skills and my ability to listen and understand others. I will work on being more open and transparent in my interactions with others, and I will strive to be a good listener and show genuine interest in their perspectives and opinions. I will also seek opportunities to practice and develop my skills, such as participating in team-building activities or taking on new projects that will challenge me to use this competency differently. By focusing on these areas, I can build and maintain relationships with others more effectively.

Teamwork Questions

During our employment, most of us will need to work in a team, ranging from a small unit of two or three people to a larger group. A person should not have to manage more than fourteen individuals, as there would not be enough time to devote to each team member. The smaller the team, the more time a manager can spend with their team members. A team's success is in the interest of everyone, and it should perform better than the sum of its parts. A great team consists of people with diverse talents that complement each other. An interviewer may already know the team's attributes for which they are recruiting and will seek to determine whether you possess the necessary complementary traits. Simply stating that you are a good team player is insufficient, as it is required to define what this entails.

Q: Tell me about when you had to get people to work together more supportively. What caused the initial difficulties? How did the others respond to you? What would you do differently next time?

A: One time, I was working on a group project in college, and there were some initial difficulties with communication and coordination. We were all very busy with other tasks and commitments, so it was hard to find when everyone could meet in person. I realized that we needed to establish more precise and consistent communication channels. So, I suggested we set up a group chat and a shared document to track our progress and discuss any issues.

At first, some group members resisted the idea, but I explained my reasoning and emphasized the importance of teamwork. Gradually, everyone started participating more actively in the chat and contributing to the document. We also checked in with each other regularly and offered help and support where needed.

Looking back, I could have been more proactive in addressing the communication issues from the beginning. If I had reached out to each group member individually and asked for their input, we could have come up with a solution more quickly. However, I was happy with the result and proud of how we could collaborate more supportively.

Q: In what past situations have you been most influential in teamwork? What did you specifically do that was effective?

A: I have been most effective as a team member in several situations, and I would like to share one example with you.

One of the teams I worked on was tasked with developing a new product for our organization. The team comprised members from different departments with diverse backgrounds and expertise. The project was complex and challenging, requiring high collaboration and coordination.

I was part of this team and contributed to the project's success in several ways. First, I actively participated in team meetings and discussions and shared my ideas and suggestions. I also listened to the ideas and suggestions of other team members, and I considered their perspectives and needs. I also provided support and guidance to my colleagues, and I helped them to overcome the challenges and obstacles they were facing.

Second, I took on additional responsibilities and tasks and volunteered to lead some sub-teams and sub-projects. I worked closely with my colleagues and manager, developing and implementing effective plans and strategies. I also monitored and reported on the project's progress and identified and addressed any issues or risks.

Third, I built strong and positive relationships with my colleagues and promoted collaboration and teamwork. I fostered a friendly and supportive environment and encouraged open communication and feedback. I also recognized and appreciated the contributions of my colleagues, and I celebrated our successes and achievements together.

Overall, this experience showed my ability to be an effective team member and contribute to the team's success and the project. I am always willing to work with others and to support and collaborate with them to achieve our goals.

Q: Tell us about the last time you worked as a team. What did you like about working in the group? What did you dislike?

A: In my previous job, I worked on a project with a team of six other people. I liked working in the group because everyone had unique skills and expertise, which helped us tackle the project from various angles. We all had different ideas and perspectives, which led to some fascinating discussions and ultimately enabled us to develop a well-rounded solution.

One thing that I disliked was the fact that sometimes it was difficult to coordinate everyone's schedules, especially when we needed to have in-person meetings. We all had different responsibilities and deadlines, which made it challenging to find a time that worked for everyone. However, we overcame this by being flexible and finding alternative methods of communication, such as email or video conferencing, when needed.

Overall, I enjoyed working in the team and appreciated the opportunity to learn from my colleagues and contribute my ideas to the project.

Q: In which situations were you least effective as teamwork? What did you do that detracted from effectiveness? What could you have done differently?

A: I have been the least effective team member in a few situations, and I would like to share one example with you.

One of the teams I worked on was tasked with developing a new marketing campaign for our organization. The project was complex and challenging, requiring high collaboration and coordination. The team comprised members from different departments with diverse backgrounds and expertise.

I was part of this team and struggled to contribute to the project's success. I was not engaged and motivated and did not participate actively in the team meetings and discussions. I was not very interested in the project, and I did not share my ideas and suggestions. I also did not listen to other team members' ideas and suggestions or consider their perspectives and needs.

I also did not take on additional responsibilities and tasks or volunteer to lead sub-teams and sub-projects. I did not work closely with my colleagues and manager nor develop and implement effective plans and strategies. I also did not monitor and report on the progress of the project and did not identify and address any issues or risks.

Furthermore, I did not build strong and positive relationships with my colleagues, and I did not promote collaboration and teamwork. I did not foster a friendly and supportive environment or encourage open communication and feedback. I also did not recognize and appreciate the contributions of my colleagues, and I did not celebrate our successes and achievements together.

Overall, this experience showed my lack of effectiveness as a team member and my failure to contribute to the team's and the project's success. I learned from this experience and tried to improve my teamwork skills and attitude and become a more valuable and supportive team member.

Q: Think of someone who's a particularly effective team player – what do they do exactly?

A: I have worked with many influential team players and would like to share one example.

One of my colleagues is a particularly effective team player who stands out for her contributions and attitude. She is always engaged and motivated and participates actively and constructively in team meetings and discussions. She shares her ideas and suggestions and listens to other team members' ideas and suggestions. She also considers their perspectives and needs and provides support and guidance.

She works closely with her colleagues and manager, developing and implementing effective plans and strategies. She also monitors and reports on the project's progress and identifies and addresses any issues or risks. She also takes on additional responsibilities and tasks and volunteers to lead sub-teams and sub-projects.

Furthermore, she builds strong and positive relationships with her colleagues and promotes collaboration and teamwork. She fosters a friendly and supportive environment and encourages open communication and feedback. She also recognizes and appreciates her colleagues' contributions and celebrates our successes and achievements.

Overall, this colleague is a particularly effective team player, and she sets a high standard for others to follow. She is an asset to the team and contributes to the team's success and the project. I am proud to work with her and learn from her example and attitude.

Q: What makes a supportive team? Why do you think this is important? What can be done to encourage people to work together more supportively? What gets in the way of successful team working?

A: A supportive team is one where members collaborate and communicate effectively to achieve shared goals. In such a team, members are willing to help each other, share ideas, and provide constructive feedback. Supportive teamwork is critical to success in any organization, as it allows individuals to leverage their strengths and collectively tackle challenges.

Creating an environment that fosters trust, respect, and open communication is essential to encourage people to work together more supportively. This can be achieved through team-building activities, regular check-ins, and creating a culture that values collaboration over competition. Additionally, it's crucial to establish clear roles and responsibilities, ensure that everyone knows the team's objectives, and encourage active participation from all members.

Several factors can hinder successful teamwork, such as poor communication, a lack of trust, and unclear goals or expectations. Conflict and personality clashes can also be barriers to effective teamwork. As a team member, it's important to actively work to overcome these obstacles by listening to others, being open to feedback, and approaching challenges with a positive and collaborative mindset.

Continuous Improvement Questions

If you apply for a job in any company, you will most likely be asked about "continuous improvement." Continuous improvement is a philosophy that involves making incremental gains for the organization by looking for changes in how people do things or processes are performed. Large companies have departments dedicated to continuous improvement using "lean thinking" and "just in time" approaches. To survive, organizations must increase or maintain their profits. Even non-profit organizations must make a difference in their field to justify their existence. There are only three ways to improve profits: sell more, sell at a higher price, or spend less on operations. Employees can contribute to reducing the cost of operations, which is the easiest way to contribute to the company's success.

Modern organizations recognize that every employee can contribute to the company's success, regardless of their role. Each employee should add value in some way and contribute to the improvement of the business. Candidates should be prepared to provide examples of how they challenged the status quo and made even the smallest gains, demonstrating their ability to contribute to continuous improvement.

Q: Tell us about when you initiated an improvement at work.

A: In my previous role, I noticed that our team spent much time manually inputting data into our project management software. It was tedious and time-consuming, taking away from more important work. I decided to research if there was a more efficient way to input the data and found a software tool that could automate the process. I presented my findings to my manager and the team, and after some discussion, we decided to invest in the tool. I took the lead in implementing the new tool and training the team. As a result, we reduced the time spent on data input by 50%, allowing us to focus on more value-added tasks. The team was pleased with the improvement; we could complete projects more efficiently.

Q: Tell us how you usually cope with a lot of work. Where do you start? What do you do to ensure it all gets done? What prevents you from getting it all done?

A: When faced with much work, I start by assessing the priority of each task and creating a to-do list. It is helpful to break down larger projects into smaller, manageable tasks and assign deadlines for each. This helps me stay organized and ensures that I am making progress toward completing everything.

I prioritize my time and work on the most urgent or important tasks to ensure everything gets done. I also take breaks throughout the day to avoid burnout and maintain productivity. Additionally, I communicate with my team and colleagues to ensure we are all on the same page and working towards the same goals.

A few things can prevent me from getting everything done, such as unexpected interruptions or changes in priorities. However, I am flexible and adapt to changes as they arise while focusing on completing my tasks as efficiently and effectively as possible.

Q: Where do you want to be in five years?

A: I have grown professionally and personally within the company in five years. I am always eager to learn new things and take on new challenges, so I plan to take on more responsibilities and roles within the company. Ideally, I would love to be in a leadership position to help guide and mentor other employees to achieve their goals. This company has a lot of growth potential, and I want to be a part of that growth by contributing to the company's success. Ultimately, I want to continue developing my skills and knowledge to be a valuable asset to the company and achieve personal satisfaction in my career.

Q: Which is more important: creativity or efficiency? Why?

A: When it comes to creativity versus efficiency, both are important and can be complementary to each other. Creativity is crucial for generating new ideas and finding innovative solutions to problems, while efficiency is essential for executing those ideas and solutions effectively. Without creativity, a company may become stagnant and fall behind competitors, while without efficiency, ideas may never become a reality or take too long to implement.

However, the importance of creativity or efficiency can vary depending on the situation. For example, in a fast-paced startup environment, imagination may be more important initially to generate unique ideas and attract investors. At the same time, efficiency may become more important to ensure sustainable growth and profitability. On the other hand, in a more established and mature company, efficiency may be more important to streamline processes and improve productivity while allowing room for creativity to drive innovation. Ultimately, it's about finding the right balance between the two and adapting to the needs of the specific situation.

Q: Tell us about a time when you have had to identify the fundamental cause of a problem. How did you solve the problem? What processes did you adopt to identify the critical cause? What lessons did you learn?

A: In my previous job, we experienced a significant decline in customer satisfaction ratings. As part of the customer service team, it was my responsibility to investigate the root cause of this issue. To identify the key reason, I started by reviewing all the customer feedback we had received, both positive and negative, and identified common themes and patterns. I also spoke to my colleagues in other departments to gain their perspectives and to see if they had any ideas about what could be contributing to the issue.

After analyzing call data, we realized that most calls were coming in during certain times of the day, leading to increased wait times. To solve this problem, I proposed a shift in scheduling to ensure that we had more staff available during peak times. I also implemented an email tracking system to ensure that all inquiries were responded to promptly. Through this process, I found that most negative feedback was related to long wait times on the phone and delayed responses to email inquiries.

As a result of these changes, customer satisfaction ratings improved significantly. I learned from this experience that a data-driven and collaborative approach could lead to more effective problem-solving.

Q: Tell us about a situation where you have implemented a process you didn't initially agree with.

A: One situation where I had to implement a process that I didn't initially agree with was when I was working on a project with a team of colleagues. We had to follow a specific process that did not align with my beliefs or preferences. The process was [specific process, such as a method of organizing the work, a way of communicating with stakeholders, etc.]. I initially disagreed with the process because [specific reasons why you opposed it, such as it was inefficient, it was not aligned with our goals, etc.]. However, I realized that the process was [specific reasons why you changed your mind, such as mandated by the company, supported by the team, etc.]. Therefore, I decided to [specific actions or strategies that you took to implement the process, such as communicating the importance of the process to the team, providing training and support, monitoring and evaluating its effectiveness, etc.]. As a result of my efforts, the team was able to [specific positive outcomes, such as adopting the process, improving their performance, etc.]. I learned from this experience the importance of being flexible, adaptable, and professional in implementing strategies that I didn't initially agree with.

Q: Describe the last time you had to analyze a lot of information or data. What sort of information did this involve? How did you pick out the essential information from the less relevant? What did you learn from the analysis?

A: The last time I had to analyze a lot of information or data was when I was [specific situation or context, such as working on a research project, conducting a market analysis, etc.]. I faced a large amount of information or data that was [specific characteristics of the information or data, such as complex, diverse, voluminous, etc.]. I knew I needed to analyze the information or data to [specific desired outcome, such as finding insights, making decisions, etc.]. I took the following steps to analyze the information or data: [specific actions or strategies you took to analyze it, such as organizing and filtering it, applying statistical methods, using visualization tools, etc.]. As a result of my analysis, I could [specific positive outcomes, such as finding the insights I was looking for, making the decisions I needed to make, etc.]. I am proud of this achievement, demonstrating my ability to analyze large amounts of information or data effectively.

Q: Give us a recent example of when you were faced with a complex problem. What made it difficult? What key steps did you take to resolve the issue? What did others think of your approach?

A: A recent example of when I faced a complex problem was working on a project with a team of colleagues. The project was [specific characteristics of the project, such as challenging, innovative, meaningful, etc.]. We were facing a problem that was [specific characteristics of the problem, such as difficult to solve, critical to the success of the project, etc.]. The problem was [specific problem, such as a technical issue, a logistical challenge, etc.]. I knew we needed to solve the problem to [specific desired outcome, such as completing the project, achieving our goals, etc.]. However, the problem was complex because [specific reasons why the situation was complicated, such as it involved multiple factors, it required specialized knowledge, etc.]. I took the following steps to solve the complex issue: [specific actions or strategies you took to solve the problem, such as gathering information and data, consulting with experts, brainstorming solutions, etc.]. As a result of my efforts, we were able to [specific positive outcomes, such as finding a solution, implementing it successfully, etc.]. I am proud of this achievement and believe it demonstrates my ability to solve complex problems effectively.

Q: Describe when you had to organize a new process/plan or project implementation. What key stages did you work through? On what basis did you determine your priorities? How did this work out in practice?

A: One time I had to organize the implementation of a new process/plan or project was when working on a team of colleagues. We were tasked with implementing a new process/plan or project that was [specific characteristics of the process/plan or project, such as complex, innovative, important, etc.]. I knew we needed to organize the implementation to [specific desired outcome, such as completing the process/plan or project on time, achieving our goals, etc.]. Therefore, I took the following steps to organize the implementation: [specific actions or strategies you took to manage the implementation, such as defining the scope and objectives, creating a timeline and budget, assigning roles and responsibilities, etc.]. As a result of my efforts, we were able to [specific positive outcomes, such as implementing the process/plan or project successfully, meeting or exceeding our goals, etc.]. I am proud of this achievement, and it demonstrates my ability to organize the implementation of new processes/plans or projects effectively.

Q: Even the most organized individuals may overlook some of the activities required in planning new activities/initiatives. Tell us about a time when this happened to you. What were the consequences of this? How did you rectify this? What was the outcome?

A: One time I overlooked some of the activities required in planning new activities/ initiatives was when working on a project with a team of colleagues. We were tasked with designing a new activity/initiative that was [specific characteristics of the activity/initiative, such as complex, innovative, important, etc.]. I thought I had planned the activity/initiative well but later realized I had overlooked [specific activities that you missed, such as a key stakeholder, a critical step, etc.]. This oversight caused [specific problems or challenges you faced, such as a delay, a misunderstanding, etc.]. I knew I needed to address the oversight to [specific desired outcome, such as completing the activity/initiative on time, achieving our goals, etc.]. Therefore, I took the following steps to address the oversight: [specific actions or strategies you took to address the oversight, such as communicating the situation to the team, identifying the root causes, proposing solutions, etc.]. As a result of my efforts, we were able to [specific positive outcomes, such as overcoming the problems or challenges, completing the activity/initiative successfully, etc.]. I learned from this experience the importance of being thorough, detailed, and flexible in planning new activities/initiatives. I also learned the value of continuously monitoring and reviewing the plan to identify and address potential oversights.

Q: Give an example of when you had to organize a piece of work, project, or event. How did you prepare and plan for it? What timescales did you set? How well did it go?

A: One time I had to organize a piece of work, project, or event was when I was working on a team of colleagues. We were tasked with managing a [specific type of work, project, or event, such as a research study, a marketing campaign, a conference, etc.]. I knew we needed to organize the work, project, or event to [specific desired outcome, such as completing it on time, achieving our goals, etc.]. Therefore, I took the following steps to organize the work, project, or event: [specific actions or strategies that you took to organize the work, project, or event, such as defining the scope and objectives, creating a timeline and budget, assigning roles and responsibilities, etc.]. As a result of my efforts, we were able to [specific positive outcomes, such as completing the work, project, or event successfully, meeting or exceeding our goals, etc.]. I am proud of this achievement, demonstrating my ability to organize work, projects, or events effectively.

Q: Give an example of when you had to work to an important deadline. How manageable were your timescales? What did you do to ensure that the deadline was met? What did you learn?

A: One time when I had to work to an important deadline was when I was working on a project with a team of colleagues. We were tasked with completing a project that was [specific characteristics of the project, such as complex, innovative, important, etc.]. I knew we needed to work to an important deadline to [specific desired outcome, such as submitting the project on time, achieving our goals, etc.]. The deadline was [specific characteristics of the deadline, such as tight, critical, etc.]. Therefore, I took the following steps to work to the urgent deadline: [specific actions or strategies you took to work to the deadline, such as prioritizing tasks, delegating work, managing resources and time, etc.]. As a result of my efforts, we were able to [specific positive outcomes, such as completing the project on time, meeting or exceeding our goals, etc.]. I am proud of this achievement and believe it demonstrates my ability to work to important deadlines effectively.

Q: Describe the last time you missed a deadline. Why did this happen?

A: The last time I missed a deadline was when working on a project with a team of colleagues. We were tasked with completing a project that was [specific characteristics of the project, such as complex, innovative, important, etc.]. The deadline was [specific characteristics of the deadline, such as tight, critical, etc.]. I had planned to complete the project on time. Still, I missed the deadline because [specific reasons why you missed the deadline, such as unexpected challenges, unforeseen circumstances, inadequate resources, etc.]. I realized that I had [specific mistakes or shortcomings that you made, such as underestimating the time and effort required, neglecting to communicate with the team, failing to prioritize tasks, etc.]. I felt [specific emotions, such as disappointment, frustration, embarrassment, etc.]. I knew I needed to address the situation to [specific desired outcome, such as completing the project, meeting our goals, etc.]. Therefore, I took the following steps to address the situation: [specific actions or strategies you took to address the problem, such as communicating with the team, identifying the root causes, proposing solutions, etc.]. As a result of my efforts, we were able to [specific positive outcomes, such as completing the project, meeting or exceeding our goals, etc.]. I learned from this experience the importance of being realistic, prepared, and resilient in managing deadlines. I also learned the value of continuous communication and collaboration with the team to overcome challenges and achieve our goals."

Customer Service Questions

Interviewers often ask questions about customer service because it is a critical aspect of many roles, particularly those that involve interacting with customers or clients. The interviewer may want to assess the candidate's knowledge, skills, and attitude toward customer service. Customer service is crucial because it can impact a company's reputation and bottom line. Employees skilled in customer service can create positive customer experiences, leading to customer loyalty, repeat business, and positive reviews. On the other hand, employees not skilled in customer service may create negative experiences that can damage the company's reputation and lead to lost business. During an interview, the interviewer may ask the candidate about their previous experience with customer service, how they would handle a demanding customer, or how they prioritize customer needs. The candidate's responses can reveal their ability to communicate effectively, solve problems, and handle challenging situations. A candidate who demonstrates strong customer service skills is likelier to be a good fit for roles that involve interacting with customers or clients.

Q: Tell me about a recent situation when you had to build a relationship with a new customer.

A: In my previous job as a sales representative, I was assigned a new customer who had just started their business and needed our services. I reached out to them via email and phone, introducing myself and asking if we could set up a meeting to discuss their needs. During our meeting, I listened carefully to their requirements and concerns and identified how our services could help them achieve their goals.

I followed up with them promptly after the meeting, answering any questions they had and providing additional information they needed. I also kept in touch regularly, sending them relevant industry news and updates and checking in to see how their business was doing.

As a result of my efforts, the customer was delighted with our services and continued to work with us long-term. Building a solid relationship with the customer helped me understand their needs better and also helped me provide better service and identify opportunities for upselling and cross-selling.

Q: Give me an example of when you have given excellent customer service.

A: In my previous job as a customer service representative for an online retailer, I received a call from a customer who needed help with a product they had purchased. The customer was very frustrated and upset, but I remained calm and empathetic as I listened to their concerns. I apologized for their experience and assured them we would do everything possible to resolve the issue.

I took the time to understand the problem thoroughly and researched possible solutions. After discussing these options with the customer, we agreed on a course of action. I followed up with the customer throughout the process to keep them informed and updated on the status of their issue.

Ultimately, we resolved the issue to the customer's satisfaction, and they even left a positive review of their experience. This situation taught me the importance of active listening, empathy, and persistence in providing excellent customer service.

Q: What, in your view, makes it difficult to relate well to certain customers?

A: Relating well to customers is critical to any customer service role, but it can sometimes be challenging. In my experience, the most common difficulty in relating to certain customers is when they are upset or frustrated. It can be tough to remain calm and empathetic when a customer is angry or has had a negative experience with the company. It can also be challenging to relate to customers with different communication styles or cultural backgrounds, as they may have different expectations and preferences for how they want to interact. It's essential to be mindful of these potential barriers and try to overcome them by listening actively, being patient, and adapting communication styles to match the customer's preferences.

Q: How much contact have you had with customers? What do you like about dealing with them? What do you dislike?

A: I have had significant contact with customers throughout my career. In my current role, I interact with customers in person and over the phone daily. I am responsible for addressing their concerns and questions and providing them with information about our products and services. I have also worked on several customer service projects, where I helped improve the customer experience and increase customer satisfaction. Overall, I have a great deal of experience working with customers and providing them with the support they need.

Q: Give an example of when you put a customer first. What sacrifices did you have to make? What impact did this have on your other activities? How did others view this?

A: One time, a customer came into our store having trouble finding the right product for her needs. She was getting frustrated and was about to leave without making a purchase. I could tell she was struggling, so I took the time to listen to her and ask questions to understand her needs better. I found the perfect product for her and even gave her a discount to show her that we value her business. She ended up smilingly leaving the store and even thanked me for my help. I was happy that I could put the customer first and ensure she had a positive experience with our company.

Q: Tell me about the last time a customer made an excessive or unreasonable demand on you. What made them so demanding? What did you do to assist them? How much time did this take?

A: The last time a customer made an excessive or unreasonable demand on me was when I worked in a call center. I received a call from a customer who was upset about a billing error and demanded that I fix it immediately. However, the error was not something that could be fixed right away and required further investigation. The customer became increasingly angry and started yelling at me, even though I was trying to explain the situation to them. I remained calm and professional and assured the customer that I would do my best to resolve the issue as quickly as possible. I followed up with the customer the next day and resolved the billing error to their satisfaction.

Q: Tell me about a time when you kept your promise to a customer, even though it was tough.

A: One time, I promised a customer that I would deliver their order by a specific date, even though I knew it would be a tight deadline. The customer relied on receiving the order by that date, so I committed to them and assured them that it would be delivered on time. I worked closely with my team and put in extra effort to ensure the order was completed and shipped on time. We met the deadline, and the customer was pleased and grateful.

Q: Describe a time when you were unable to help out a customer as much as they wanted. Why was this? What did they say about your reaction? What did your manager say?

A: There was also a time when I was unable to help out a customer as much as they wanted. A customer came to me with a problem outside my expertise and looking for a solution. I did my best to help them, but I could not give them the answer they were looking for. I apologized for not being able to assist them further and offered to connect them with someone who might be able to help them. The customer was disappointed, but I did my best to handle the situation honestly and empathetically.

Q: Tell me about when you were complimented for helping a customer beyond the call of duty. How frequently do you go into that kind of situation? What other similar feedback have you received?

A: Once, I received a compliment for helping a customer beyond the call of duty. I worked at a clothing store, and a customer came looking for a particular item. I could not find it in the store, but I remembered seeing it in a catalog. I went above and beyond my usual duties and called another store to see if they had the item in stock. I found the item and even arranged delivery to the customer's home. The customer was very grateful and thanked me for going the extra mile to help them. My manager also complimented my excellent customer service and dedication to helping our customers.

Q: Give an example of when you had to listen very carefully to a customer. What did they tell you? How did you check that you had grasped all the information? How did you show you were listening?

A: One time, I had to listen very carefully to a customer to help them with their problem. I was working in a call center and received a call from a customer having trouble with their account. They were babbling and very upset, so I had to listen carefully to understand their issue and provide the correct information. I stayed calm and focused and asked them questions to clarify their problem. I could give them the help they needed and resolve the issue to their satisfaction. The customer was grateful and thanked me for my patience and understanding.

Q: Describe a situation in which you have dealt with an irate customer. Why were they angry? How did you begin to calm them down?

A: I have dealt with a particularly angry customer several times, but one situation stands out. I was working in a retail store, and a customer came in yelling and cursing because they were upset about a product they had purchased. They demanded to speak to a manager and were very aggressive and hostile. I stayed calm and tried to de-escalate the situation by listening to the customer's concerns and apologizing. I offered to refund their money or replace the product, and the customer eventually calmed down and accepted my offer. I was able to resolve the situation and prevent it from escalating further.

Q: What are the key factors influencing a customer's first impression? Why do you think they are important?

A: The appearance and cleanliness of the location, including the storefront, signage, and interior.

The friendliness and professionalism of the staff, including their greeting, attitude, and appearance.

The quality and variety of products or services offered and their presentation.

The speed and efficiency of service, including the time it takes to be greeted, served, and checked out.

The overall atmosphere of the location, including the lighting, music, and smells.

The availability and accessibility of information, including product descriptions, prices, and policies.

The convenience of the location, including the parking, hours, and payment options.

Influencing Skills Questions

In most organizations, the ability to get things done through others is based on our capacity to influence them rather than giving them direct orders. Although companies may have a hierarchical structure, the reality is that changes are usually initiated through individuals with different viewpoints and persuade others to make the necessary changes. However, this does not mean no decisions are made through a "chain of command." These decisions are typically strategic or tactical rather than day-to-day operations.

Even if your role is not directly related to sales or marketing, your ability to influence others is still essential to your job. For instance, in production, you may need to convince maintenance personnel to stop production for proper maintenance. On the other hand, we are all influenced by our colleagues and superiors at work without requiring formal orders. Therefore, your capacity to influence others will likely be an essential factor in the job you are applying for, whether explicitly stated in the job description or not.

Q: What are your strengths in terms of influencing people? What's your approach to influencing others? What could you do to make yourself more effective in influencing others?

A: Regarding influencing others, my strengths are building rapport and establishing trust with people. I take the time to listen to their perspectives and understand their needs, and then work to find common ground and solutions that benefit everyone involved. My communication skills are also strong, which helps me to articulate my ideas and persuade others clearly and concisely.

My approach to influencing others is identifying what motivates them and their priorities. Understanding their perspective allows me to tailor my message and approach to resonate with them and speak to their interests. I also provide evidence and data to support my arguments, as I believe facts can be persuasive in making a case.

I could continue working on my active listening skills and understanding others' viewpoints to make myself more effective in influencing others. Building relationships and networks across different teams and departments is essential. This can help me understand the dynamics and identify potential allies in making changes or influencing decisions. Finally, I would seek feedback from others on improving my influencing skills, as there is always room for growth and development.

Q: Give an example of when you had to settle a dispute between two people.

A: In my previous role, two team members had a dispute over a project they were working on together. The disagreement was causing tension and impacting team morale. I decided to meet with them separately to understand their perspectives and concerns. Through active listening and asking open-ended questions, I got to the issue's root and identified common ground. I then facilitated a meeting between the two team members, where they could discuss their concerns openly and find a solution that worked for both of them. I ensured that both parties had a chance to express their thoughts and feelings and that the conversation was respectful and productive. Ultimately, they reached a mutually beneficial agreement and continued working together effectively. I learned that it's crucial to approach conflict resolution with empathy and patience and to create a safe space for all parties to express their thoughts and feelings.

Q: Have you ever had a conflict with a superior? How was it resolved?

A: Yes, I have had a conflict with a superior. During a project, I had a different opinion from my manager on our approach. I had researched and felt that my suggested approach was the better option, but my manager disagreed and wanted to go in a different direction. We met to discuss our differing views, and I listened actively to my manager's perspective and understood their concerns. I then presented my argument clearly and concisely, providing evidence to support my reasoning. Ultimately, we reached a compromise that satisfied both of us and allowed us to proceed successfully with the project. What helped to resolve the conflict was our willingness to listen to each other's perspectives and be open to alternative ideas. We both focused on what was best for the project rather than on our egos or opinions.

Q: Some people are easier to persuade than others. What is it that makes persuading them so difficult? Which people do you find hard to convince?

A: People who are very set in their ways and have a strong attachment to their current beliefs or methods can be challenging to persuade. These individuals often have much experience and knowledge in their expertise, making them resistant to change or alternative ideas. To persuade them, it's important to approach the conversation with respect for their expertise and to explain the reasoning behind the proposed change carefully. It's also important to listen actively and thoughtfully to address their concerns. Building trust and credibility with these individuals can take time, but persuading them effectively is necessary.

Q: Tell me about the last time you won someone over to your point of view. How did your opinion contrast with their original position? What were the key things that you did which persuaded them? What kind of agreement did you reach?

A: The last time I won someone over my point of view was when I was working on a team project, and we had to decide which approach to take. Some of my teammates were in favor of one approach, while others were in favor of a different approach. I favored a third approach and had to convince my teammates to adopt my perspective.

I started by listening carefully to their points of view and trying to understand their reasoning. I then presented my perspective, explaining the reasons behind my recommendation and addressing any concerns or objections they had. I also provided evidence and examples to support my point of view and offered to answer any questions or give more information.

Through this process, I was able to win some of my teammates over to my point of view. They agreed that my approach had merits and would most effectively achieve our goals. We were able to move forward with my recommendation and complete the project.

Overall, winning someone over your point of view requires effective communication, empathy, listening, and understanding of others' perspectives.

Q: Give a recent example of when you negotiated a successful outcome. What did you negotiate? How did you win the person round? How did you know that they were convinced?

A: I recently negotiated a successful outcome when trying to buy a car. I had found a car that interested me, but the price was higher than I was willing to pay. I decided to negotiate with the seller to get a better price.

I started by doing some research on the car and its market value so that I had a good understanding of what a fair price would be. I then approached the seller and explained that I was interested in the car but that the price was higher than I was willing to pay. I suggested a lower price and explained why I believed it was fair.

The seller countered with a slightly higher price, and we went back and forth negotiating until we reached a mutually acceptable price. I got the car at a price I was happy with, and the seller made a profitable sale for them.

Successful negotiation involves effective communication, understanding the other party's perspective and interests, and being willing to compromise to reach a mutually beneficial outcome.

Q: Give an example of a time when you could not persuade someone around to your point of view. Why was this important? Why did you not succeed? What have you learned?

A: I have been unable to persuade someone around to my point of view occasionally, but one situation stands out. I was working on a team project, and we had to decide which approach to take. I favored one approach, but one of my teammates vehemently opposed it and advocated for a different approach.

I tried to persuade the teammate by explaining the reasons behind my recommendation and addressing any concerns or objections. I also provided evidence and examples to support my point of view and offered to answer any questions or give more information. However, the teammate opposed my approach and was unwilling to consider my perspective.

In the end, we were unable to reach a consensus and had to compromise by adopting a different approach which was a compromise between the two options. I was disappointed that I failed to persuade my teammate to my point of view, but I learned that sometimes it is impossible to convince someone to change their mind and that it is essential to be willing to compromise to move forward.

Q: There are times when no one is prepared to listen or agree with a point of view. Give an example of when this happened to you. How did you present your view/idea? What were their objections? How hard did you push your viewpoint? Where did you leave the conversation?

A: There have been times when no one was prepared to listen or agree with my point of view, but one situation stands out in my mind. I was working on a team project, and we had to decide which approach to take. I favored one approach, but all of my teammates vehemently opposed it and advocated for a different approach.

I tried to explain my perspective and the reasons behind my recommendation, but no one was willing to listen. They shut down my ideas and were not open to considering my point of view. I felt frustrated and frustrated that I was not being heard.

In the end, we were unable to reach a consensus and had to compromise by adopting a different approach which was a compromise between the two options. I was disappointed that my point of view was not considered, but I learned that sometimes it is impossible to convince others to agree with you and that it is crucial to adapt and find a solution that works for everyone.

Q: For most of us, the occasion arises when we must convince others to make an unpopular choice/decision. Give an example of when you have had to do this. How did you try to get others on board? What was the result? With hindsight, how could you have approached this differently?

A: I have had to convince others to make an unpopular choice or decision several times, but one situation stands out. I was working in a customer service role and received a call from a customer who was extremely upset about a billing error. I tried to resolve the issue, but the customer was not satisfied with my response and continued to escalate the situation.

I realized the situation would not be resolved to the customer's satisfaction, so I escalated the issue to my manager. My manager agreed with my assessment and decided that the best course of action would be to issue a credit to the customer's account. However, this was an unpopular decision because it meant the company would have to absorb the cost of the error.

Even though it was unpopular, I had to convince my coworkers and supervisors to support the decision. I explained the situation and the reasons behind the decision and provided evidence to support my argument. I also addressed their concerns or objections and offered to answer any questions. Through this process, I convinced the others to support the decision and move forward with issuing the credit.

Overall, I believe that convincing others to make an unpopular choice or decision requires effective communication, empathy, and the ability to listen and understand others' perspectives. It also requires persistence and overcoming objections and resistance to reach a positive outcome.

Q: What kind of correspondence/presentations have you had to produce in the past? How frequently have you had to write this kind of work? How was it received?

A: I have had to produce various correspondence and presentations as part of my professional work and academic studies. For example, I have had to write emails, memos, reports, and proposals in various professional settings. I have also had to prepare presentations using tools such as PowerPoint and deliver those presentations to groups of people.

In addition, I have had to produce academic papers, essays, research proposals, and presentations as part of my studies. These have required me to conduct research, analyze data and information, and present my findings in a clear and organized manner.

Overall, I have experience producing a wide range of correspondence and presentations and have developed strong writing, research, analysis, and presentation skills. These skills are essential for anyone working in a professional or academic setting, and I am confident in my ability to produce high-quality correspondence and presentations.

Q: Tell me about your experience in preparing reports/documents. How often have you had to prepare reports? How do you go about it? What do you do particularly well?

A: I have experience preparing reports and documents in various professional and academic settings. For example, I have had to write reports and proposals as part of my work in marketing, where I had to analyze data and information and present my findings in a clear and organized manner. I have also had to prepare academic papers and research proposals as part of my studies, which required me to conduct research, analyze data and information, and present my findings clearly and concisely.

In addition, I have experience using software tools such as Google Docs and Sheets to create and edit reports and documents. I have also developed strong research, analysis, and writing skills, which have helped me produce high-quality reports and documents.

Overall, my experience in preparing reports and documents has given me the skills and knowledge necessary to create and edit professional and academic documents effectively. I am confident in producing high-quality reports and clear, concise, well-organized documents.

Q: For many businesses, good communication is crucial to success. What factors, in your view, ensure good communication? What advice might you give to someone struggling with their communication? How might you improve your own written communication? What steps have you taken to do this?

A:

- *Clear and concise language: Good communication involves using clear, concise, and easy-to-understand language. It is essential to refrain from jargon or technical terms that may be difficult for others to understand.*

- *Active listening: Good communication involves listening to what others say and paying attention to their words, tone, and body language. It is essential to show that you are listening to provide feedback and asking clarifying questions when necessary.*

- *Empathy and understanding: Good communication involves understanding the perspective and needs of the other person and being able to put yourself in their shoes. Being empathetic and showing that you care about the other person's feelings and concerns is essential.*

- *Nonverbal cues: Good communication involves using nonverbal cues such as body language and facial expressions to convey meaning and to show that you are engaged and interested in the conversation. It is essential to be aware of your nonverbal cues and to pay attention to the nonverbal cues of others.*

These factors are essential for ensuring good communication, and I strive to incorporate them into my communication style.

Q: In what situations do you find it challenging to get your point across? Why is this so? What do you do to overcome these difficulties? What methods have you observed others use?

A:

- *When the other person is not listening or paying attention: Sometimes, it can be challenging to get your point across if the other person is not listening or paying attention to what you are saying. They may be distracted by other things, or they may be focused on their thoughts and ideas. Engaging the other person and making them listen to your perspective can be challenging.*

- *When the other person is resistant or unwilling to listen: Sometimes, the other person may be resistant or unwilling to listen to your perspective, either because they disagree with you or have preconceived ideas and beliefs. In these situations, persuading the other person to consider your perspective can be challenging. You may need different approaches and tactics to get your point across.*

- When there is a language or cultural barrier: Sometimes, there may be a language or cultural barrier that makes it challenging to communicate effectively. For example, suppose you are speaking to someone who does not speak your language fluently or sharing with someone from a different culture. In that case, you may have to use more straightforward language or adapt your communication style to be understood.

Overall, these are some situations in which it can be challenging to get your point across. I try to be aware of them to communicate effectively in any situation.

Q: Think of one of your colleagues whom you consider to be very influential. How does your style differ from theirs? Give an example of your approach.

A: One of my colleagues I consider very influential is _____. _____ is a confident and assertive person who is not afraid to speak her/him mind and express her/his opinions. They are persuasive and can convince others to support their ideas and proposals.

In contrast, my style is more reserved and analytical. I prefer to listen and observe before speaking and tend to be more measured and thoughtful in my approach. I also value collaboration and teamwork, and I consider the perspectives and ideas of others before making decisions.

Overall, our styles are different, but they both have their strengths and weaknesses. I admire _____ confidence and assertiveness, and I try to learn from her/him to improve my communication and leadership skills. At the same time, my more reserved and collaborative style can be helpful in certain situations and that it complements _____ style well.

Q: Tell us about a situation when you had to modify your plans/actions to account for other people's views. What was the problem? How did the other people express their views?

A: I have had to modify my plans or actions to account for other people's views on several occasions. For example, I was once working on a team project, and we had to decide which approach to take. I had a strong preference for one approach, but some of my teammates were in favor of a different approach.

I listened carefully to their perspectives and tried to understand their reasoning. Their approach had some merits and could benefit certain aspects of the project. I decided to modify my plan and incorporate elements of their approach into my own.

This required me to be flexible and adapt my plan to account for their views. I also had to communicate and collaborate with my teammates to integrate their ideas and create a plan acceptable to everyone.

Overall, this situation showed my ability to be flexible and to adapt my plans to take account of others' perspectives. I am willing to modify my plans or actions to achieve a positive outcome, and I value collaboration and teamwork in achieving our goals.

Q: How do you get your boss/others to accept an idea?

A:

- *Present the idea clearly and concisely: I present the idea clearly and concisely, using language that is easy to understand. I also provide examples or evidence to support my argument and address potential objections or concerns.*

- *Listen to others' perspectives: I try to listen to others' perspectives and understand their reasoning and concerns. I also try to ask clarifying questions and provide feedback to ensure everyone is on the same page.*

- *Be open to feedback and suggestions: I am available for feedback and suggestions from others and consider their ideas and perspectives. Collaboration and teamwork are essential for achieving success, and I am willing to modify my ideas to incorporate the views of others.*

- *Communicate the benefits and value of the idea: I communicate the benefits and value of the concept and show how it can benefit the organization or the team. I also explain why the idea is important and worth considering and provide evidence or examples to support my argument.*

Change Management Questions

Nowadays, the concept of "continuous improvement" is becoming more prevalent among various organizations. This philosophy embraces change as an essential element, which can be adopted by some but not all individuals. While some people view change positively as enhancing their work experience, others may feel anxious and resist it, overtly or subtly. During a job interview, you may be asked about your experiences with change in the workplace, including instances where you initiated or led change. This does not necessarily refer to formal change management programs but rather any simple changes you made to your work approach that benefited the organization. You may also be asked how you reacted to the change imposed on you. Since change is inevitable in organizations as they develop and grow, it is crucial to be prepared to provide responses that showcase your adaptability and willingness to embrace change.

Q: Tell us about a recent time you had to adapt to a significant change. How did you adapt? What was difficult about the transition?

A: Recently, there was a significant change in our company's workflow process. We were transitioning from a manual process to an automated one, which involved many changes to our daily routine. I had to adapt to this change quickly, as my team was responsible for the timely completion of specific tasks in the process. To adapt to the change, I first tried to understand the new system thoroughly by attending training sessions and reading manuals provided by the company. I also contacted colleagues with prior experience with the new system to learn them. One of the difficulties I faced was adjusting to the new terminology used in the design, as it differed from what we were used to. Another challenge was the initial slowdown in our team's performance as we got used to the new system. However, I stayed positive and motivated my team to learn and adapt. Eventually, we adjusted to the changes and improved our performance. This experience taught me the importance of being adaptable and proactive in the face of change.

Q: Tell us about a recent time when you questioned or challenged a way of working. Why did you ask it? What alternative did you suggest? To what extent were your ideas used?

A: In my previous job, I noticed that our team spent much time manually updating a specific report weekly. It was a tedious process that took up much valuable time that could have been spent on more strategic tasks. I decided to speak up and suggest an alternative approach that would automate the report and save us significant time.

I brought up my concerns to my manager and suggested using a software program that I had experience with that could automatically generate the report for us. I demonstrated how the software worked and showed how it could eliminate the need for manual data entry and formatting. My manager was initially hesitant to make the switch because of the cost of the software and the time it would take to set it up. However, I made a strong case for the potential long-term benefits and showed how the time saved in the long run would offset the software cost.

Eventually, my ideas were adopted, and we successfully implemented the new system. The transition period was challenging because we had to learn how to use the latest software and adapt to a new way of working, but we worked together as a team to overcome any issues that arose. In the end, we significantly reduced the time spent on the report and used that time for more impactful work.

Q: Describe an occasion when you had to change how you work because of changing circumstances. What were the main changes in terms of demands? What was your initial reaction? How well did you adapt?

A: One occasion I had to change how I work because of changing circumstances was when I was working on a project with a tight deadline. Initially, I planned to work independently and complete the project independently. However, as the deadline approached, I realized that the project's scope was more extensive than I had anticipated and that I would need help to finish it on time. I quickly adapted my approach and asked my colleagues for assistance. Together, we could divide the work and complete the project successfully, despite the unexpected challenges and changes. I learned from this experience that being flexible and adaptable is critical to staying on track and achieving success, even when faced with unexpected changes.

Q: Give an example of a time when you had to change your work plans unexpectedly. What was your first reaction? How did you change your plans? What was the outcome?

A: There was a time when I was working on a project that required me to collaborate with a colleague from another department. We had a clear timeline and work plan, but unexpectedly, my colleague had to go on sick leave for several weeks. At first, my initial reaction was to feel overwhelmed and unsure of how to proceed. However, I quickly realized I had to adapt my plans to ensure the project remained on track.

I re-evaluated the work plan and identified areas where I could progress without my colleague's input. I also reached out to other colleagues who had similar expertise and could help fill the gap left by my colleague's absence. Additionally, I communicated with our project manager to update them on the situation and get their input on how to proceed.

As a result of these changes, we were able to complete the project on time and within budget, despite the unexpected absence of my colleague. This experience taught me the importance of being adaptable and proactive in facing unforeseen challenges and reinforced the value of effective communication and collaboration with colleagues and supervisors.

Q: Describe when you needed to explain an unexpected change in work plans to colleagues. What was their reaction? How did you manage their adaptation?

A: One time when I needed to explain an unexpected change in work plans to colleagues was when I was working on a project with a tight deadline. I had planned to complete the project in a certain way and had a detailed schedule and timeline. However, as I was working on the project, I encountered [unexpected challenges or changes, such as new information, changing requirements, unexpected delays, etc.]. I needed to adapt my plans to meet the deadline and ensure the project's success. I quickly reassessed the situation and developed a new program that would [specific actions or strategies that would address the challenges or changes]. I then met with my colleagues to explain the differences and discuss the new plan. I made sure to listen to their feedback and address any concerns they had. I was able to implement the new plan successfully, with the support and collaboration of my colleagues. I learned from this experience the importance of communication and cooperation in managing unexpected changes in work plans.

Q: Suggestions for change often come from the unlikeliest of sources. Tell us about a time when this has happened to you. What was the catalyst for change? What was your reaction? How did you manage your colleagues" reactions? What was the outcome?

A: One time when a suggestion for change came from an unlikely source was when I was working on a project with a team of colleagues. I had planned to complete the project in a certain way and had a detailed schedule and timeline. However, one of my colleagues, who was new to the team and unfamiliar with the project, suggested a different approach that I had not considered. Initially skeptical of the suggestion, I decided to listen and consider it carefully. After some discussion and consideration, I realized that the proposal was a good one and would improve the project's efficiency and effectiveness. I decided to incorporate the suggestion into the plan, and I completed the project successfully, thanks in part to the contribution from this unlikely source. I learned from this experience the value of being open to ideas and suggestions from all sources, regardless of their level of knowledge or expertise.

Q: Give us a recent example of when you came up with a different approach/ solution to a situation or problem. What suggestions did you make? Which ideas were put into practice? What was the outcome?

A: A recent example of when I came up with a different approach/solution to a situation or problem was working on a project with a team of colleagues. The project was facing some challenges, and we were struggling to find a way to move forward. I decided to step back and look at the situation from a different perspective. I realized that the traditional approaches we had been using were not working and that we needed to try something new. I devised a process involving [specific actions or strategies different from the traditional approaches]. I presented my idea to the team, and we tried it. The new approach worked well, and we overcame the challenges and completed the project successfully. I learned from this experience the value of thinking outside the box and being willing to try new approaches to solve problems and achieve success.

Q: Describe a crisis at work that you have had to handle recently. What caused it? What did you do to resolve it?

A: One crisis at work that I recently had to handle was when one of our key suppliers experienced significant disruption in their operations. This disruption caused a delay in the delivery of the necessary materials that we needed for one of our projects. I was responsible for managing the project, and I knew the delay would significantly impact our timeline and our ability to meet our customer commitments. I quickly assessed the situation, and I came up with a plan to mitigate the impact of the delay. I contacted our other suppliers to see if they could provide the needed materials, and I worked with our team to develop alternative solutions and contingency plans. I also communicated with our customers to inform them of the situation and reassure them that we were doing everything possible to keep the project on track. Despite the challenges, we successfully navigated the crisis and completed the project on time. I learned from this experience the importance of being proactive, adaptable, and communicative in managing crises and unexpected challenges in the workplace.

Q: In what past situations have you been most effective at motivating others through periods of change? What did you do specifically that was effective? What supportive conditions were present?

A: In the past, I have been most effective at motivating others through periods of change when I have [key factors or strategies that contributed to your success, such as communicating clearly and openly, providing support and guidance, demonstrating my commitment and enthusiasm, etc.]. One example was when I led a team through a [specific type of change, such as a restructuring, a merger, a technology upgrade, etc.]. I knew this change would be challenging for the team, and I wanted to ensure they remained motivated and engaged throughout the process. I took the following steps to motivate them: [specific actions or strategies that you took to motivate the team, such as holding regular meetings to update them on the progress of the change, providing training and resources to help them adapt to the new situation, recognizing and celebrating their achievements, etc.]. As a result of these efforts, the team successfully navigated the change and performed at a high level. I am proud of this achievement, demonstrating my ability to motivate others through periods of change.

Q: Think of someone who's particularly effective in motivating others – what do they do exactly?

A: The person who is particularly effective in motivating others that I can think of is [name]. I have observed [them] in action and how [they] can motivate others to achieve their best. [They] does this in several ways, including [specific actions or *strategies that the person uses to encourage others, such as providing clear goals and expectations, giving constructive feedback, recognizing and rewarding their achievements, etc.]. [They] also have [specific personal qualities or characteristics that contribute to [their] success in motivating others, such as enthusiasm, passion, empathy, etc.]. Overall,[they] are particularly effective in motivating others because [they] can [key reasons why [they] is adequate, such as connect with them, inspire them, support them, etc.]. I have learned a lot from [them], and I strive to apply [their] approach to motivate others.*

Business Acumen Questions

Upon seeing a section dedicated to commercial awareness, you may think it's not your responsibility and that other professionals like accountants and finance controllers handle it. However, it's crucial to have commercial awareness regardless of the industry and position you work in. A company's success is critical for survival, and every employee somehow impacts its bottom line. Therefore, you should be able to demonstrate how you contribute and show an understanding of the "bigger picture." Even if you plan to work for a non-profit organization, it's essential to consider cost-cutting measures to make the most of the available funds.

Q: Why, in your opinion, do customers choose our products and services?

A: Customers choose your products and services because they see value in what you offer. They believe your products or services will meet their needs or solve their problems better than your competitors. Your brand has a reputation for quality, reliability, and customer service that customers trust. Additionally, customers choose your products and services because of their unique features and benefits and how they differentiate from the competition. It's essential to understand what sets your products and services apart from others in the market and communicate that effectively to potential customers.

Q: How could we make our products more competitive?

A: To make your products more competitive, there are a few key areas to focus on. Firstly, you could invest in research and development to improve the quality of your products, making them more durable and efficient than your competitors. This could involve conducting customer surveys to find out what features or improvements they would like to see in your products.

Secondly, you could focus on price competitiveness by looking at ways to reduce costs in your production process without sacrificing quality. This could involve negotiating better deals with suppliers, optimizing your supply chain, or implementing more efficient manufacturing processes.

Thirdly, you could explore ways to enhance the customer experience, such as providing exceptional customer service, offering extended warranties or guarantees, or providing additional services or products that complement your core offerings.

Overall, by taking a strategic approach to product development, cost optimization, and customer service, you can make your products more competitive in the marketplace and gain a stronger foothold against your competitors.

Q: What are the market trends that affect us?

A: Several market trends impact your industry, and any company needs to monitor them closely. One significant trend is the growing demand for sustainable and eco-friendly products. Consumers are increasingly concerned about the environmental impact of their products, and companies that can offer greener options are likely to see increased demand. Another trend is the rise of e-commerce and online shopping, which has disrupted traditional retail channels and changed how people shop. Companies that can adapt to this trend by offering convenient and seamless online experiences will likely be more competitive. Finally, there is the digitalization trend, with more companies leveraging technology to improve their operations and customer experiences. By keeping up with these market trends and adapting to them, your company can stay ahead of the curve and remain competitive in the long run.

Q: What opportunities have you had to identify cost savings in the past?

A: In my previous role as a project manager at XYZ Company, I was tasked with reducing project expenses without compromising quality. One approach I took was to analyze our procurement process to identify potential cost savings. I noticed that we were ordering some materials at a higher cost than what was available in the market. After researching and negotiating with suppliers, I found alternative vendors who could provide the same materials at a lower price without sacrificing quality. This initiative resulted in a savings of approximately 15% on our project budget. Additionally, I proposed consolidating some of our vendors to streamline the procurement process, which resulted in a further 5% cost savings. Overall, my ability to identify cost-saving opportunities helped our team to complete projects on budget and maintain profitability.

Q: How did you choose where to make the savings?

A: When identifying areas for cost savings, I thoroughly analyze the organization's financial statements and identify areas where expenses can be reduced without negatively impacting the quality of the product or service. Once I've identified potential areas for savings, I work with relevant stakeholders and team members to gather insights and data to understand the impact of any proposed changes on the business operations. During this process, I also consider potential risks and evaluate each option's benefits and drawbacks before deciding where to make the savings. Ultimately, the goal is to ensure that the cost-saving measures are sustainable and won't negatively impact the product or service quality.

Q: How much money do you think you saved?

A: When I identified cost-saving opportunities in my previous role, I tracked the savings carefully to ensure accuracy. I always strive to identify cost-saving opportunities that are feasible and have a significant impact on the company's finances. In one instance, I was able to negotiate a better contract with a vendor, which saved our company $125,000 over the course of a year. In another example, I recommended changing our office supply ordering process, resulting in a monthly savings of $2,300.

Q: Why, in your opinion, do customers choose our products and services? What benefits do they have for the customer? How could we make them more competitive? How could we make them more profitable? What are the market trends that affect us?

A: Customers choose your products and services because they are known for their positive attributes, such as quality, innovation, reliability, etc.]. Customers are also drawn to your company because of your commitment to [important principles or values, such as sustainability, customer service, diversity, etc.]. Additionally, your customers appreciate your offering [unique or differentiating factors, such as a wide range of products, personalized service, competitive pricing, etc.]. Overall, customers highly regard your products and services and choose you because of your reputation, values, and unique offerings.

Q: In what way do you think the role for which you are applying contributes to our overall business performance? How could we measure this impact?

A: The role for which I am applying contributes to our overall business performance by [key contributions, such as improving efficiency, increasing revenue, enhancing customer satisfaction, etc.]. My [relevant skills, experience, and knowledge] will enable me to [specific actions or tasks that will contribute to the business performance]. Additionally, I am committed to [important principles or values that align with the company's goals and objectives], enabling me to be a *valuable and influential team member. Overall, I can significantly contribute to the company's performance and success in this role.*

Q: What is the most important thing you have done to take account of costs/ profits/commercial value? What prompted you? What long-term impact did you have? How could you have increased this further?

A: The most important thing I have done to take account of costs, profits, and commercial value was when I was responsible for [task or project]. In this situation, I [specific actions or strategies you took to consider costs, profits, and commercial value]. For example, I [specific examples of actions or decisions that demonstrated your focus on prices, profits, and commercial value]. As a result of these efforts, I was able to [positive outcomes, such as reducing costs, increasing profits, improving customer value, etc.]. This experience taught me the importance of considering these factors in my work, and I am committed to prioritizing them in my future endeavors.

Q: Give an example of a time when you spotted a good business opportunity. What was it? Why did you think it was worthwhile? What was the outcome?

A: One time I spotted a good business opportunity was when working as a [position or job title], and I noticed a [market need or demand] that needed to be met. I did some research, and I discovered that [critical information that supported the opportunity]. I then worked with my team to develop a [product or service] that would [specific benefits or solutions that the product or service would provide]. We were able to [positive outcomes, such as secure funding, launch the product, generate revenue, etc.]. I am proud of this achievement, demonstrating my ability to identify and capitalize on promising business opportunities.

Q: What general commercial factors do you think are most critical in managing the financial performance of any area of business?

A: The most critical commercial factors in managing the financial performance of any area of business are [key factors such as revenue, costs, competition, market trends, etc.]. These factors are essential because they [specific reasons why these factors are critical, such as determining a business's profitability, providing insight into the market, enabling the company to adapt to changing conditions, etc.]. It is also important to consider [additional factors, such as customer satisfaction, innovation, efficiency, etc.] to [positive outcomes, such as maintaining a competitive advantage, improving financial performance, etc.]. Overall, these commercial factors are crucial to the success of any business, and they should be carefully managed and monitored to achieve the best financial performance.

Personal Growth And Mentoring Questions

Questions about personal growth and mentoring are often asked during interviews for various reasons. Firstly, they want to understand the candidate's mindset and values toward professional development and growth. How candidates answer these questions can reveal their motivation, ambition, and willingness to learn and improve. Additionally, companies often prioritize the development of their employees, and having a growth mindset is an essential trait for success in many roles. Interviewers may ask about personal growth and mentoring to assess whether the candidate fits the company's culture and values. Moreover, if the company has an established mentoring program, the interviewer may want to know if the candidate is interested in participating and taking advantage of such opportunities. Demonstrating an interest in personal growth and mentoring during an interview can make candidates stand out and increase their chances of being hired.

Q: What would you consider to be your development needs?

A: I believe everyone has areas for improvement, and I'm no exception. One of the areas that I'm currently working on improving is my public speaking skills. While I'm comfortable presenting to small groups, I want to become more effective at presenting to larger audiences. To address this, I've enrolled in a public speaking course and have been practicing my skills by giving to my team and colleagues whenever possible.

Another area for development that I've identified is my proficiency in a particular software program that is commonly used in the industry. While I have some experience with it, there is still much to learn regarding its advanced features and capabilities. To address this, I have started exploring online resources, such as tutorials and forums, to improve my knowledge and skills.

Overall, I'm always looking for ways to improve myself professionally, whether it's through training, mentorship, or on-the-job experience. I believe continuous learning and development are crucial to success in any role, and I'm committed to ongoing improvement.

Q: What do you consider to be your weaknesses?

A: One of my weaknesses is that I tend to be too much of a perfectionist, which can sometimes lead to spending too much time on a task or project, even if it's unnecessary. While attention to detail is essential, I have learned to balance it with practicality and efficiency, and I am constantly working on improving my time management skills. Another area where I have identified weakness is public speaking, as it can be challenging to speak confidently in front of a large audience. However, I have been actively seeking opportunities to develop and practice this skill, such as joining a public speaking club, attending workshops, and volunteering to present at work meetings. I believe that self-awareness and a willingness to improve are vital in addressing weaknesses and becoming a better professional.

Q: In what past situations have you been most effective in developing others?

A: In my previous role as a team leader, I had the opportunity to develop my team members' skills and abilities. One situation that stands out is when I identified a team member struggling with a specific task. Rather than simply taking over the job, I sat with the team member and discussed their approach. I provided them with additional resources and support and worked with them to develop an improvement plan. Over time, the team member's performance improved significantly, and they could take on more challenging tasks.

Another situation where I was influential in developing others was during a company-wide training program. I took on the role of a mentor and worked closely with a group of new employees to help them understand the company culture and processes. I provided guidance and feedback and helped them develop their communication, teamwork, and problem-solving skills. By the end of the program, the new employees were fully integrated into the team and could contribute effectively to the company's goals.

Q: What can you do to become more effective in developing other people? Where are you most effective in attracting and developing the talent of others? What behaviors should you practice more/less?

A:

- *Provide regular feedback and guidance: I can provide regular feedback and guidance to others to help them understand their strengths and weaknesses and to support their growth and development. I can also offer constructive criticism and suggestions for improvement to help others learn and grow.*

- *Encourage and support learning and development: I encourage others to learn and develop new skills and knowledge. I can provide opportunities for learning and development, such as training or mentoring, and I can provide support and resources to help others grow and achieve their goals.*

- *Model good behavior and practices: I can model good behavior and practices and serve as a positive role model for others. I can demonstrate the values and standards I expect from others and show how to apply those values and standards in practice.*

- *Foster collaboration and teamwork: I can foster cooperation and teamwork and create a positive and supportive environment that encourages others to learn and grow. I can also encourage others to share their ideas and perspectives and to work together to achieve common goals.*

Overall, these are some practical ways to become more effective in developing other people, and I am committed to incorporating them into my leadership and management style.

Q: In what situations have you succeeded in furthering your personal development? How did you do this? What risks did you take?

A: In my previous role, I wanted to develop my skills in project management, so I took the initiative to ask my supervisor if I could shadow her during a large-scale project. She agreed, and I observed her decision-making process, communication strategies, and project-planning methods. I also took an online course in project management to supplement my knowledge. After a few months, my supervisor entrusted me with smaller projects to manage independently, allowing me to practice my new skills. Regarding risks, I was initially nervous about asking to shadow my supervisor and take on new responsibilities. Still, I recognized that it was necessary for my personal and professional growth. It paid off in the end, as I successfully managed these smaller projects and gained confidence in my abilities as a project manager.

Q: Tell me about a situation where you felt you failed in your personal development. Why do you think it happened? What have you learned from this?

A: I once felt I failed in my personal development when I did not prioritize my learning and growth. I was so focused on meeting my work and personal responsibilities that I did not make time for my development. As a result, I fell behind in my field, and I did not have the skills or knowledge to stay competitive and advance in my career.

I realized that I had to make a change, and I started to prioritize my personal development. I began seeking new learning opportunities and setting aside time for personal growth and development. I also sought feedback and guidance from others, using that feedback to improve my skills and performance.

Over time, I regained my momentum and caught up with my peers. I acquired new skills and knowledge and enhanced my personal and professional growth. I learned the importance of prioritizing my development, and I have continued to focus on learning and growth to stay competitive and advance in my career.

Overall, this experience taught me the importance of prioritizing my personal development and making time and effort to learn and grow. I am committed to pursuing opportunities for learning and growth and making my personal development a priority in my life.

Q: Describe a recent opportunity you had to take on new responsibilities. How did the opportunity arise? What were the new responsibilities? What was the outcome?

A: I recently had the opportunity to take on new responsibilities when my manager asked me to lead a new project for our team. This project was a significant undertaking, and it involved coordinating the efforts of several groups across the organization.

I accepted the challenge, and I began to work on developing a plan for the project. I coordinated with other teams to identify their needs and allocate resources, and I created a timeline and budget for the project. I also worked closely with my manager to ensure the project aligned with our team's goals and objectives.

I faced many challenges and obstacles throughout the project but overcame them through hard work and collaboration. I brought the project to a successful conclusion and received positive feedback from my manager and other teams.

Overall, this opportunity allowed me to take on new responsibilities and show my leadership and management skills. I was able to learn and grow, and I was able to contribute to the success of the project and the organization. I am grateful for the opportunity and look forward to new challenges and responsibilities.

Q: When did you last learn a new skill (at work)? What was it? How did you apply your learning? What feedback did you receive about your performance?

A: The last time I learned a new skill at work was when I took a training course on project management. I had been interested in learning more about project management for some time and heard that this course was highly recommended.

I decided to take the course and spent several weeks learning about the principles and practices of project management. The course covered topics such as project planning, risk management, and stakeholder engagement, and it provided practical tools and techniques that I could apply in my work.

I found the course informative and engaging, and I could apply what I learned to my work immediately. For example, I could use the tools and techniques I learned in the course to develop a more effective project plan for a project I was working on. I also received positive feedback from my manager and from other team members, who noticed an improvement in my project management skills.

Overall, this experience showed my willingness and ability to learn and apply new skills to my work. I am always looking for opportunities to learn and grow, and I value my organization's support and resources for learning and development.

Q: What example can you give us where you have supported and encouraged a colleague? What did you do? What did they need? What was the result?

A: Several times, I have supported and encouraged a colleague and would like to share one example with you.

One of my colleagues was working on a complex project, and she needed help with some of the technical aspects of the project. She was feeling overwhelmed and frustrated and considering giving up on the project.

I saw that she was struggling, and I offered to help her. I spent some time with her, discussing the project and brainstorming solutions to the challenges that she was facing. I also provided her with some resources and guidance and offered to review her work and provide feedback.

Over time, I saw her confidence and her performance improve. She was able to overcome the challenges that she was facing, and she was able to complete the project successfully. She was grateful for my support and encouragement and thanked me for helping her stay motivated and focused.

Overall, this experience showed my willingness and ability to support and encourage a colleague. I am always happy to help others and value collaboration and teamwork in achieving our goals.

Q: Describe a situation in which you have faced a problematic individual. How did you handle this?

A: I have been faced with a problematic individual several times, and I would like to share one example with you.

One of my colleagues was very difficult to work with. He was always negative, critical, and unwilling to listen to others or consider their perspectives. He was also very demanding and inflexible, making it difficult for others to work with him.

I found this situation challenging and struggled to maintain a professional and respectful relationship with this colleague. However, I knew it was essential to find a way to work with him, so I tried to understand his perspective and find a way to communicate with him effectively.

I started by listening to and asking him questions to understand his concerns and needs. I communicated clearly and concisely and provided him with the needed information and support. I also tried to be flexible, compromise, and find solutions to meet his and the team's needs.

Over time, I was able to build a better relationship with this colleague and work with him more effectively. He became more open and receptive to my ideas and more willing to collaborate and work together. We were able to achieve our goals and complete our projects successfully.

Overall, this experience showed my ability to handle difficult individuals and find ways to work with them effectively. I am always willing to listen and understand others and to find ways to communicate and collaborate with them.

Q: Describe how your current role has changed/developed over the years.

A: My current role has changed and developed significantly over the years. When I started in this role, my responsibilities were limited to a few specific tasks, and I did not have much autonomy or decision-making authority. I was mainly focused on completing my tasks and meeting my deadlines, and I did not have the opportunity to learn or grow.

However, over the years, my role has changed and expanded. I have taken on new responsibilities and challenges and have been given more autonomy and decision-making authority. I have learned and developed new skills and knowledge, and I have been able to apply them to my work. I have also been able to contribute to the success of the team and the organization and take on a leadership role.

My role is much broader and more complex today than when I first started. I am responsible for many tasks and projects, making many decisions and solving complex problems. I have to work with many different teams and stakeholders, and I have to manage my own time and resources effectively.

Overall, my current role has changed and developed significantly over the years, and I am grateful for the opportunities and challenges it has provided me. I look forward to learning, growing, and positively contributing to the team and the organization.

Q: Tell me about your professional style and how it has developed/changed over the years. Has there been a time when it was inappropriate, and you had to adapt it?

A: My professional style has developed and changed over the years as I have gained experience and learned new skills. When I started my career, I was focused on completing my tasks and meeting my deadlines, and I was not very confident in my abilities or decisions. I was primarily reactive and did not take many initiatives or risks.

However, over the years, I have become more confident and proactive. I have learned to take on new challenges, take the initiative, make decisions, and solve problems. I have also learned to be more adaptable, flexible, and effectively work with others. I have also known to be more strategic and forward-thinking and think about my actions' long-term implications.

Today, my professional style is more balanced and mature. I can combine my technical and problem-solving skills with my leadership and management abilities. I can take on complex and challenging projects and lead and motivate others. I can communicate effectively and build strong relationships with colleagues, clients, and stakeholders.

Overall, my professional style has developed and changed over the years, and I am proud of the progress that I have made. I always seek ways to learn, grow, and develop my professional style and abilities.

Q: Give us an example of a time when you were unfairly criticized about something. Why was this? How did you respond? What was the outcome?

A: I have been unfairly criticized several times and would like to share one example with you.

One of my managers criticized me for a mistake I made in a project I was working on. The error was minor, and it did not have any significant impact on the project. However, my manager was furious and upset and criticized me in front of my colleagues and clients. She accused me of being competent and not taking my work seriously and threatened to take disciplinary action against me.

Her criticism shocked and hurt me; I felt it was unfair and unjustified. I worked hard on the project, avoided mistakes, and delivered high-quality work. I also communicated openly and honestly with my manager and clients and informed them about the error as soon as I discovered it.

I decided to defend myself and explain my side of the story to my manager and my clients. I showed them the evidence and the facts and explained how the mistake had happened and how I had addressed it. I also apologized for the error and offered to take responsibility and make amends.

My manager and my clients listened to me, and they understood my perspective and my actions. They agreed that the criticism was unfair and unjustified and praised me for my professionalism and integrity. They also apologized for the complaint and thanked me for contributing to the project.

Overall, this experience showed my ability to handle unfair criticism and defend myself and my work. I am always willing to accept constructive criticism and learn from my mistakes, but I am also ready to stand up for myself and defend my reputation and values.

Leadership Skills Questions

At some point in their career, many individuals are promoted and take on the responsibility of overseeing others' work as well as their own. Climbing the corporate ladder is often the only way people measure success in their chosen careers. However, other methods of measuring career success have yet to be entirely accepted. Therefore, in this chapter, any role involving leading others is considered positive. The answers provided below are written from the perspective of someone who has previously led others. It can be challenging for someone who has never held a leadership position to convince others of their leadership skills. However, by understanding the underlying principles in the answers, individuals can adapt their responses to include phrases such as "If I were in that situation, I would have…"

Q: Describe when you had to coordinate other people's work. What were you trying to achieve? How did you go about organizing the work?

A: In my previous role as a project manager, I had to coordinate the work of a cross-functional team to develop a new product for our company. The objective was to launch the product promptly and efficiently while ensuring all stakeholders were aligned and satisfied with the outcome.

To organize the work, I first set clear objectives for the project and identified the key deliverables that needed to be completed. I then met with each team member individually to assign tasks and clarify their responsibilities. I also established a communication plan to ensure that everyone was aware of project updates and could address any issues or concerns promptly.

I held regular team meetings throughout the project to monitor progress and identify areas needing additional attention. I also supported team members when necessary and facilitated collaboration between different departments.

As a result of this coordination, we successfully launched the product on time and within budget. The team also established better communication and collaboration, which helped improve overall efficiency and effectiveness.

Q: Think of someone who is particularly effective in providing leadership. What do you think they do successfully?

A: In my experience, influential leaders have a few key traits in common. Firstly, they are great communicators and can clearly articulate their vision and goals to their team. They also actively listen to their team members and provide regular feedback to help them grow and develop. Secondly, they lead by example and are not afraid to get their hands dirty when needed. They work alongside their team members to demonstrate their commitment and dedication. Finally, influential leaders are adaptable and open to new ideas. They can pivot and make changes as needed to achieve the desired outcome. Effective leaders inspire and motivate team members to reach their full potential while driving results.

Q: Describe a time when your input motivated others to reach a team goal. Why was this necessary? What did you do to motivate the team? Why did this work?

A: In my previous role, we had a tight deadline to complete a project, and the team was feeling overwhelmed and demotivated. I knew we needed to come together and get everyone focused and energized to meet the deadline. To do this, I scheduled a team meeting and started by acknowledging everyone's hard work and progress so far, which helped to boost morale. I then shared my vision for completing the project on time, outlining each team member's responsibilities and how their contributions would be crucial to our success. I also listened to everyone's concerns and ideas, which helped build trust and strengthen our working relationships. Throughout the project, I regularly checked in with team members to provide encouragement and support and recognized and celebrated milestones. This approach helped to motivate the team, and we completed the project on time.

Q: Describe a time when you successfully helped someone carry out a task independently. How did you enable them to carry out the work? How did you follow this up? What was the outcome?

A: I successfully helped someone carry out a task independently when working with [name], a [colleague/employee/student, etc.]. [They] was [specific situation or challenge, such as new to the team, struggling with a particular task, etc.]. I knew that [they] needed help to [specific desired outcome, such as improve [their] skills, complete the task successfully, etc.]. I decided to [specific actions or strategies that you took to help [them] carry out the task independently, such as providing training and resources, giving clear instructions and expectations, offering support and guidance, etc.]. As a result of my efforts, [they] were able to [specific positive outcomes, such as improving [their] skills, completing the task successfully, becoming more confident and independent, etc.]. I am proud of this achievement, demonstrating my ability to independently help others carry out tasks.

Q: Describe a situation when you found it challenging to focus the work of a team on an objective. What made this work difficult? How did you try to overcome these difficulties? How could you improve upon this?

A: One situation when I found it challenging to focus the work of a team on an objective was when I was leading a group of colleagues on a project. The project aimed to [specific goal, such as develop a new product, improve a process, etc.]. However, the team faced some challenges and distractions that prevented them from focusing on the objective. These challenges included [specific challenges, such as conflicting priorities, lack of resources, changing requirements, etc.]. I found it challenging to keep the team focused on the objective because [specific reasons why it was difficult, such as the challenges were overwhelming, the team was not united, etc.]. I took the following steps to address the situation: [specific actions or strategies that you took to help the team focus on the objective, such as clarifying the goal and its importance, providing support and resources, aligning the team's efforts, etc.]. As a result of my efforts, the team was able to [specific positive outcomes, such as overcoming the challenges, increasing their productivity, improving their morale, etc.]. We were able to reach our goal on time and with high quality. I learned from this experience the importance of being proactive, persistent, and supportive in helping a team focus on an objective.

Q: What opportunities have you had to identify development opportunities for others? What action did you take? Why was this important? What impact did this have?

A: I have had many opportunities to identify development opportunities for others in my career. For example, [specific examples of opportunities you have had, such as in my role as a manager, in my participation in a mentoring program, etc.]. In these situations, I have [specific actions or strategies that you have taken to identify development opportunities for others, such as assessing their strengths and areas for improvement, providing feedback and guidance, offering training and resources, etc.]. As a result of my efforts, I have helped many individuals [specific positive outcomes, such as improving their skills, advancing in their careers, achieving their goals, etc.]. I am passionate about helping others develop, and I believe my ability to identify development opportunities is integral to my contribution to their success.

Q: We all have times when we find it difficult to control the activities of others. Give an example of when you faced this type of situation. Why did you find the situation challenging? How did you overcome the difficulties you faced?

A: One time I faced a situation where I found it difficult to control the activities of others was when I was working on a project with a team of colleagues. The project was complex, requiring coordination and collaboration among the team members. However, some team members were not following the plan and were not completing their tasks on time. I found it difficult to control their activities because [specific reasons why it was difficult, such as they were not responsive to my requests, they were not accountable for their actions, etc.]. I took the following steps to address the situation: [specific actions or strategies you took to help the team members control their activities, such as setting clear expectations and deadlines, providing support and resources, holding them accountable for their performance, etc.]. I learned from this experience the importance of being firm, fair, and supportive in helping others control their activities. As a result of my efforts, the team members achieved [specific positive outcomes, such as improving their performance, increasing their productivity, etc.]. We were able to complete the project on time and with high quality.

Q: In what past situations have you been most effective in providing leadership and direction? What did you specifically do that was effective? What supportive conditions were present? In which cases were you least effective? What could you have done differently?

A: In the past, I have been most effective in providing leadership and direction when I have [key factors or strategies that contributed to your success, such as communicating clearly and openly, setting clear goals and expectations, demonstrating my commitment and integrity, etc.]. One example was when I led a team through a [specific type of situation, such as a project, a challenge, a change, etc.]. I knew the team needed strong leadership and direction to [specific desired outcomes, such as succeeding in the situation, achieving their goals, etc.]. I took the following steps to provide leadership and direction: [specific actions or strategies you took to lead and direct the team, such as setting the direction and priorities, providing support and guidance, recognizing and celebrating their achievements, etc.]. As a result of my leadership and direction, the team was able to [specific positive outcomes, such as overcoming the challenges, increasing their productivity, improving their morale, etc.]. I am proud of this achievement and believe it demonstrates my ability to provide leadership and direction.

Q: In what situations have you been most influential in empowering others? What did you do that was incredibly effective? What results did you see?

A: In the past, I have been most effective in empowering others when I have [key factors or strategies that contributed to your success, such as listening to their needs and concerns, providing support and resources, recognizing and rewarding their achievements, etc.]. One example was when I was working with a group of colleagues who were [specific situation, such as new to their roles, facing a challenging project, etc.]. I knew that they had the potential to be [specific desired outcome, such as more confident, more skilled, more productive, etc.]. However, they needed support and guidance to achieve [specific desired outcome, such as improving their skills, overcoming challenges, etc.]. I took the following steps to empower them: [specific actions or strategies you took to empower the team, such as providing training and resources, giving clear instructions and expectations, offering support and guidance, etc.]. As a result of my efforts, they achieved *[specific positive outcomes, such as improving their skills, increasing their confidence, becoming more independent and productive, etc.]. I am proud of this achievement, demonstrating my ability to empower others.*

Specialist Knowledge Questions

The interviewer may want to assess the candidate's knowledge, experience, and qualifications in a particular technical or specialized area. Specialist knowledge is vital for the success of a business, particularly in industries such as technology, engineering, and healthcare. Employees with technical skills and expertise can provide valuable insights and contributions to the organization, leading to improved performance, innovation, and competitive advantage. During an interview, the interviewer may ask the candidate about their previous experience with specific programming languages, software, or tools related to the job. They may also ask the candidate to provide examples of projects they have worked on or how they have solved complex technical problems related to the role. The candidate's responses can reveal their expertise, problem-solving skills, and ability to apply knowledge in practical settings.

Q: How do you keep up with advances in your profession? Which specialist or technical blogs or websites do you read? How much time do you spend doing this? How do your efforts to keep up with developments compare with your peers?

A: I make a conscious effort to keep up with the advances in my profession, and I follow several strategies and practices to stay current and knowledgeable.

First, I read professional blogs, forums, and newsletters and stay updated on my field's latest trends and developments. I also follow industry leaders and experts and learn from their insights and experiences. I also attend conferences, seminars, and workshops and network with other professionals and experts.

Second, I take online courses and certifications and learn new skills and knowledge relevant to my profession. I also participate in online forums and discussions and exchange ideas and experiences with other professionals. I also seek mentorship and guidance from more experienced professionals and learn from their expertise and advice.

Third, I apply my knowledge and skills daily and challenge myself to learn and grow. I also seek feedback and advice from my colleagues and manager, using it to improve and develop. I also share my knowledge and experiences with my colleagues, and I help and support them to learn and grow.

Overall, staying up to date with the advances in my profession is crucial for my success and career growth. I am committed to continuous learning and development and always seek opportunities and resources to enhance my knowledge and skills.

Q: Tell me about when colleagues sought your technical advice or experience. Why do you think they sought your advice? How accurate was your advice? What have you done since to acquire extra knowledge?

A: I have been asked for technical advice and experience by my colleagues many times, and I would like to share one example with you.

One of the teams I worked on was tasked with developing a new software application for our organization. The team comprised members from different departments with diverse backgrounds and expertise. The project was complex and challenging, requiring high technical skills and knowledge.

I was part of this team and recognized for my technical skills and experience. Several times, my colleagues came to me for advice and support, and I was happy to help them. For example, they asked me for guidance on the design and architecture of the application, and I shared my ideas and suggestions with them. I also helped them select the appropriate technologies and tools and provided technical support and training.

Furthermore, I helped them troubleshoot and debug the application and provided them with solutions to the technical issues they faced. I also helped them to optimize and improve the performance and quality of the application, and I suggested and implemented several enhancements and improvements.

Overall, this experience showed my technical skills, experience, and ability to guide and support my colleagues. I learned from this experience and tried to share my knowledge and skills with my colleagues and contribute to the team's success and the project.

Q: Which technical problems are the most challenging for you? What are your strengths and weaknesses technically? How does your level of knowledge compare with that of your peers? What feedback have you received about it?

A: One of the most challenging technical problems for me is when there is a complex coding issue that requires a lot of debugging and troubleshooting to resolve. However, I enjoy a good challenge and always try to approach problems with a problem-solving mindset. One of my technical strengths is my ability to quickly learn new technologies and programming languages, which has been helpful in my previous roles. Additionally, I am good at breaking down complex problems into smaller, more manageable tasks, which helps me stay organized and focused.

I am still developing my skills in database management and optimization. While I have experience working with databases, I know there is always room for improvement. I have been actively seeking opportunities to learn more and improve my skills in this area. My technical knowledge is on par with that of my peers, but I also recognize that there is always something new to learn, and I am open to feedback and constructive criticism to help me grow and improve my skills. In my previous role, I received positive feedback from my colleagues and supervisors regarding my ability to troubleshoot and resolve technical issues efficiently and effectively.

Q: What methods do you choose to learn by, and why do you prefer these?

A: I prefer to learn through hands-on experience, observation, and instruction. I find that actively engaging with the material or task helps me to retain information better and develop a deeper understanding. I like to observe experts in action and learn from their techniques and approaches. Additionally, I appreciate structured instruction, such as online courses or workshops, which can provide a more organized and comprehensive approach to learning. Ultimately, I try to be flexible and adapt to the learning method most suits the situation.

Q: Give an example of when your technical/specialist knowledge helped you to solve a problem. What brought this issue to light? What did you do? What was the result of your efforts?

A: One of the projects I worked on was developing a new website for our organization. The website was a complex and dynamic platform, requiring a high level of technical skills and knowledge.

I was part of the team responsible for developing the website, and I was recognized for my technical knowledge and expertise. I was asked to solve a problem that the team was facing, which was related to the security and the performance of the website.

I analyzed the problem and the requirements and used my technical knowledge and experience to identify the root cause of the issue. I found that the problem was caused by the configuration of the website and the server and that it needed to be optimized for security and performance.

I proposed a solution to the problem, which was to redesign and implement the security and performance of the website. I used the latest technologies and tools and applied the best practices and standards in my solution. I also tested and evaluated the solution, ensuring it met the requirements and expectations.

The solution was accepted and implemented, and it helped improve the website's security and performance. The project was completed successfully and received positive feedback and praise from the stakeholders and users.

Overall, this experience showed my technical knowledge, expertise, and ability to solve complex and challenging problems. I learned from this experience and tried to enhance and apply my technical knowledge and skills.

Q: Describe a recent time when you felt that your specialist knowledge level needed improvement. What made you think this? What action did you take? What are your current strengths and weaknesses in this area?

A: One of the tasks I was assigned was to investigate and analyze a new technology emerging in my field. The technology was complex and innovative, requiring a high level of specialist knowledge and expertise.

I was excited and curious about the technology and wanted to learn more about it and its potential applications. However, as I started researching and studying the technology, I realized that my specialist knowledge level was insufficient to understand and evaluate it fully.

I found that the technology had many advanced and sophisticated features and differed from the technologies I was familiar with. I also found that the documentation and available resources were not comprehensive and clear, and I needed more knowledge and expertise to understand and apply the technology.

I felt frustrated and overwhelmed by the challenges and the gaps in my knowledge, and I thought I could not contribute and support the project as much as I wanted. I sought help and guidance from my colleagues and manager and asked them for advice and support.

They were understanding and supportive, and they helped me to learn and improve my knowledge and skills. They provided me with the resources and materials I needed and offered me the opportunity to attend workshops and seminars related to the technology.

Overall, this experience showed my willingness and ability to learn and grow and overcome the challenges and limitations of my specialist knowledge. I learned from this experience, expanded and deepened my specialist knowledge, and kept up with the latest developments and trends in my field.

Q: It can sometimes be challenging to apply the knowledge gained in specialized courses to the workplace. What opportunities have you had to do this? How did you adapt the knowledge? What was the outcome?

A: One of the specialized courses that I attended was related to project management, and it provided me with the knowledge and the skills to plan, manage, and control complex and dynamic projects. The course covered various topics, including project scope, schedule, budget, resources, risks, and stakeholders.

After completing the course, I could apply the knowledge and skills I gained to a real-world project I was working on. The project was new and challenging, requiring high coordination and collaboration among the team members and the stakeholders.

I applied the principles and techniques that I learned in the course to the project, and I used them to identify and define the objectives and requirements of the project and to create the project plan and the schedule. I also used them to monitor and control the progress and the performance of the project and to identify and resolve the issues and risks that arose during the project.

I received positive feedback and praise from my manager and colleagues for my work on the project and my ability to apply the knowledge and skills I gained in the course to the workplace. I also learned from the project and gained valuable experience and insights that helped me improve and develop my project management skills and knowledge.

Overall, this experience showed my ability and willingness to apply the knowledge and skills I gained in specialized courses to the workplace and use them to solve real-world problems and challenges. I learned from this experience and continued learning and developing my knowledge and skills and applying them to my work.

Q: How do you apply your specialist knowledge to a commercial environment? How valuable is that approach? What are the limitations of that approach?

A: As a specialist in my field, my knowledge should be applied to benefit the company's bottom line. To do this, I typically begin by familiarizing myself with the company's products, services, and goals. I then identify areas where my expertise can be utilized to improve these offerings or streamline processes. I believe it's important to communicate my ideas clearly and effectively and work collaboratively with others in the organization to ensure that my recommendations are viable and align with the company's overall strategy.

This approach is beneficial, allowing me to leverage my specialized knowledge to contribute to the organization's success. However, I am also mindful of the limitations of this approach. While my expertise can certainly be an asset, it's essential to recognize that many factors are at play in a commercial environment, including market trends, customer preferences, and competitive pressures. Therefore, I always strive to stay informed about broader industry developments and collaborate with colleagues from other departments to ensure my recommendations are well-rounded and consider these external factors.

Q: Give an example of an area where you consider yourself to have detailed knowledge or expertise. Tell me what important changes are taking place in this field. What are the implications of this?

A: One of the areas where I have detailed knowledge and expertise in data analysis and visualization. I have worked in this field for many years and have gained a deep and comprehensive understanding of the methods and techniques used to collect, process, and analyze data and present and visualize the results and insights.

I have extensively studied and practiced data analysis and visualization and have learned and applied various tools and technologies to support and enhance my knowledge and skills. I have also attended workshops and seminars and read and learned from books and online data analysis and visualization resources.

I have also had the opportunity to apply my knowledge and skills to a wide range of projects and tasks and to use them to support and enhance the decision-making and performance of the business. I have used data analysis and visualization to uncover and discover hidden patterns and trends, to identify and evaluate opportunities and risks, and to support and validate the hypotheses and assumptions of the business.

My knowledge and expertise in data analysis and visualization are valuable and essential for the company. They help drive and support its decisions and actions. I have received positive feedback and recognition from my colleagues and manager for my work and my expertise in data analysis and visualization, and I have contributed to the success and growth of the business.

Q: What professional standards have you had to adhere to in the past? Why were they necessary? What difficulties did you encounter maintaining them? How did you ensure that others also complied with these standards?

A: In my previous job as a healthcare professional, I had to adhere to several professional standards, including patient confidentiality, ethical treatment of patients, and adherence to medical guidelines. These standards were essential to ensure the safety and well-being of the patients, maintain the integrity of the healthcare profession, and comply with legal and regulatory requirements.

One difficulty I encountered in maintaining these standards was managing conflicts of interest between patients and other stakeholders, such as insurance companies or pharmaceutical representatives. To ensure compliance with professional standards, I worked closely with my colleagues and sought guidance from regulatory bodies when necessary. I also participated in ongoing education and training to stay up-to-date with changing standards and best practices.

As a team player, I encouraged my colleagues to adhere to these standards by leading by example, promoting open communication, and creating a supportive work environment. Maintaining professional standards is essential in any industry to build trust, respect, and credibility with stakeholders and to achieve success in the long term.

Brainteasers Questions

Q: Tell me ten ways to use a pencil other than writing.

Q: Sell me this pencil.

Q: If you were an animal, which one would you want to be?

Q: If you could choose one superhero power, what would it be and why?

Q: If you could choose any superpower, what would you choose and why?

Q: Why do tennis balls have fuzz?

Q: What animal would you want to be and why?

Q: Without using a scale, how would you weigh a plane?

Other Diverse Questions

Q: What would constitute a perfect evening for you?

Q: What would be a nightmare evening?

Q: Would you rather have an extremely successful professional life and have a tolerable home life or a fabulous home life and a merely tolerable professional life?

Q: If you could wake up tomorrow having gained one new ability, skill, or quality, what would it be?

Q: Who is your hero/heroine (alive or dead)?

Q: Who is your biggest villain?

Q: Describe the person who has influenced your life most.

Q: Has anyone told you that you have been their inspiration?

Q: How forgiving are you? Give me an example.

Q: Have you ever made a big sacrifice? If you have, is it something you have kept to yourself, or do others know about it?

Q: Has anyone ever made a big sacrifice for you?

Q: What percentage of people your age do you think are having a better life than you? On a scale of 1 to 10, how happy are you?

Q: Tell me about the last time you laughed at yourself.

Q: Do others laughing at you bother you?

Q: How would you describe your work style?

Q: What would be your ideal working environment?

Q: What do you look for in terms of culture—structured or entrepreneurial?

Q: Give examples of ideas you've had or implemented.

Q: What techniques and tools do you use to keep yourself organized?

Q: If you had to choose one, would you consider yourself a big-picture or detail-oriented person?

Q: Tell me about your proudest achievement.

Q: Who was your favorite manager, and why?

Q: What do you think of your previous boss?

Q: Was there a person in your career who made a difference?

Q: What kind of personality do you work best with and why?

Q: What are you most proud of?

Q: What do you like to do?

Q: What are your lifelong dreams?

Q: What do you ultimately want to become?

Q: What is your personal mission statement?

Q: What are three positive things your last boss would say about you?

Q: What negative thing would your last boss say about you?

Q: What three character traits would your friends use to describe you?

Q: What are three positive character traits you don't have?

Q: If you were interviewing someone for this position, what traits would you look for?

Q: List five words that describe your character.

Q: Who has impacted you most in your career, and how?

Q: What is your greatest fear?

Q: What is your biggest regret and why?

Q: What's the most important thing you learned in school?

Q: Why did you choose your major?

Q: What will you miss about your present/last job?

Q: What is your most outstanding achievement outside of work?

Q: What are the qualities of a good leader? A bad leader?

Q: Do you think a leader should be feared or liked?

Q: How do you feel about taking no for an answer?

Q: How would you feel about working for someone who knows less than you?

Q: How do you think I rate myself as an interviewer?

Q: you wouldn't want me to know about yourself

Q: Tell me the difference between good and exceptional.

Q: What kind of car do you drive?

Q: There's no right or wrong answer, but if you could be anywhere in the world right now, where would you be?

Q: What's the last book you read?

Q: What magazines do you subscribe to?

Q: What's the best movie you've seen in the last year?

Q: What would you do if you won the lottery?

Q: Who are your heroes?

Q: What do you like to do for fun?

Q: What do you do in your spare time?

Q: What is your favorite memory from childhood?

Q: Describe your favorite childhood memory.

Q: What do you like to do in your free time?

Q: What kind of things do you do for fun?

Q: Who are your heroes, and why?

Q: What is the first thing you would do if you were to win the lottery?

Q: What is your favorite movie that you've seen this year?

Q: Do you subscribe to any magazines? If so, which ones?

Q: Tell me about the last book that you read.

Q: Where would you go if you could travel anywhere right now?

Q: What kind of car do you drive?

Q: Describe the difference between exceptional and good.

Q: Tell me something about yourself or your past that you wouldn't want me to know.

Q: How would you rate me as an interviewer?

Q: How would you feel about being more skilled or knowledgeable than your supervisor?

Q: How do you feel about hearing "no?"

Q: Do you think leaders should be liked or feared?

Q: In your opinion, what makes a good leader?

Q: What qualities make a terrible leader?

Q: Outside of your career, what has been your greatest accomplishment?

Q: What will you miss most about your current/previous job?

Q: Why did you major in [x] in college?

Q: What is the most valuable thing that you learned in school?

Q: Tell me about your biggest regret in life.

Q: Describe what you're most fearful of.

Q: Who has had the most significant impact on your career?

Q: What are three positive qualities that you don't possess?

Q: What is something negative that your previous employer would say about you?

Q: Tell me three positive things your previous employer would say about you.

Q: What is your life's mission statement?

Q: Ultimately, what do you hope to achieve and become?

Q: Tell me about your lifelong aspirations.

Q: What do you enjoy doing?

Q: Describe what you are most proud of.

Q: *What personality types do you work well with and why?*

Q: *Is there someone that changed or altered your career path?*

Q: *How do you feel about your previous employer?*

Q: *Have you had a favorite supervisor? Why were they your favorite?*

Q: *Do you see yourself as a detail-oriented or big-picture person?*

Q: *What tools and strategies do you use to stay organized?*

Q: *Give me an example of a solution you developed or implemented at work.*

Q: *Do you prefer an entrepreneurial or structured company culture?*

Q: *Describe your perfect work environment.*

Q: *What is your work style?*

Exercise

"Why did the job candidate wear sunglasses to the interview? They wanted to be ready for a bright future!"

Too many people are anxious in anticipation of an interview. You can only do so much to make your resume stand out. However, interviews depend a lot on how well-prepared you are. If they decide to invite you for an interview, they think you have the potential! Your success during the interview will depend on 80% of your preparation level and 20% of your fit for the position. Don't underestimate the value of good preparation for an interview.

The list of questions and mainly the answers provided are there for you to know what is expected and give you a template on how to form your answers. Choose ten to twenty questions most relevant to your field and the position you seek. Then rehearse those questions aloud with a friend. Preparing the answers mentally is a good start, but it is important to practice answering aloud to make yourself comfortable with your answers and the delivery. Be sure to incorporate specific examples from your experience to demonstrate your skills and qualifications. Ask your friend to comment on your delivery, the sample you used, and how confident and optimistic you sound.

Practice, practice, practice, and good luck!

THE THRILLING SEQUEL

'The key to a successful interview is to be yourself - but at your best.' -
Susan M. Heathfield

The Technical Test

Congratulation if you get to that stage; you are very close to getting the job. This is the part where the keywords are: "Don't mess up."

At this stage, the only reason you would not get the job is if you are either too hasty or incompetent. Take your time to answer the question, and do it as if your life depends on this only "test." The correct answers are essential. But also focus on presentation, proper language, etc… This will remove any doubt your interviewer has regarding your application.

Do your test correctly, and not only do you will get the job, but you might get the recruiter existed to get you onboard.

The Right References

'The quality of your life is the quality of your relationships.' - Tony
Robbins

Your reference, by all means, needs to speak highly about you. The more important the position of your references, the better it is, as it has more weight in the recruiter's mind. A reference from the organization's CEO probably has more weight than one from the janitor. We are all influenced in some ways by titles. Try to ensure diversity in your references; if all references are all your colleagues from one job, it is less valuable than if each reference comes from people from different organizations in different positions.

When choosing references to include on your resume, consider the following tips:

- Check the job posting: Look at the job posting to see if the employer has specified any reference requirements. Some employers may only want professional references, while others prefer personal ones.

- Match the references to the job: Consider the nature of the job and the skills required. Select references who can speak to your experience and skills most relevant to the job.

- Choose recent references: Selecting references you have worked with in the past few years is best. This will give the employer a more accurate picture of your current abilities and work style.

- Get permission: Before adding someone as a reference on your resume, ensure you have their permission. This will also allow them to prepare for potential phone calls from prospective employers.

- Diversity of references: Try to include a mix of references, such as former supervisors, colleagues, or clients, to provide a well-rounded perspective of your skills and work ethic.

- Provide complete contact information: Include the name, job title, company name, email, and phone number of each reference on your resume. This will make it easier for the employer to contact them if needed.

Remember that your references can play a crucial role in helping you land a job. Therefore, it's essential to choose them thoughtfully and ensure they can provide a positive and accurate portrayal of your skills and experience.

Negotiating The Best Salary

"If you don't ask, you don't get. Negotiation is about having the courage to ask for what you want." - Sophia Amoruso

Negotiating salary can be daunting, but it's an essential part of the interview process. Knowing how to negotiate your salary effectively can significantly impact your earning potential and overall job satisfaction. Here are some tips on how to negotiate the best salary during interviews.

First and foremost, research the industry and the company to get an idea of the average salary range for the position you are applying for. This will give you a benchmark to start negotiations and ensure you are not undervalued. Secondly, it's essential to highlight your achievements and experience during the interview process. Emphasize how your skills and qualifications make you an ideal fit for the role and how they can add value to the company. This will demonstrate your worth and provide a solid foundation for negotiations.

When discussing salary, it's crucial to let the employer bring up the topic first. Don't be the first one to mention numbers, as it may put you at a disadvantage. When the employer does bring up salary, be prepared to justify why you believe you are worth the amount you request. Be flexible and open to negotiation. If the employer offers a lower salary than you were expecting, consider asking for other forms of compensation, such as a signing bonus or additional vacation days. This can help bridge the gap between what you are looking for and what the employer offers.

It's also important to remember that negotiation is a two-way street. The employer may have limitations on what they can offer regarding salary and compensation. Be willing to compromise and work together to find a mutually beneficial agreement. Lastly, consider the total package when negotiating salary. Benefits such as health insurance, retirement plans, and stock options can add significant value to your compensation package. Make sure to take these into account when negotiating.

In summary, negotiating salary can be intimidating, but you can effectively negotiate your best possible pay with proper research, preparation, and communication. Remember to be flexible and open-minded and focus on the overall compensation package, not just the base salary. With these tips, you can confidently negotiate your salary and achieve your deserved compensation.

Handling Rejection

"Don't let rejection define you. Let it refine you." - Unknown

You were confident that you had found your dream job, despite struggling to find a position matching your unique skills and abilities. After customizing your cover letter and resume to fit the recruiter's preferences, you applied and were invited for a first-round interview, which went well. When asked to return for a second-round interview and a company tour, you believed you were a finalist and began thinking about salary and benefits. However, your hopes were dashed when you received an email delivering bad news. Although this situation may seem overly dramatic, it is a common experience in the job market, given the high competition for positions. Those who have already faced job rejections can relate, and those about to enter the job market may face similar challenges. It's essential to recognize that rejection is a possibility before finding the right job.

Despite the abundance of advice about securing employment in a challenging economy, little about coping with job rejection is mentioned. Even though rejection is expected in a competitive job market, there is still a reluctance to acknowledge it. Rejection is an unpleasant reality often quantified through statistical data comparing job applicants to available positions. Post-graduate placement programs tend to emphasize the positive and encourage graduates to remain optimistic, which means that they may not prepare them for a rejection or provide guidance on dealing with negative news. It is essential to reflect on how you will respond to rejection and recognize that your reaction can be as critical as your performance during an interview.

Rejection comes in varying degrees of intensity. Receiving a rejection note after applying for a position and not making it to the interview stage may be disappointing, but it is typically manageable. The recruiter hasn't met you, so the rejection isn't personal. Additionally, you haven't been able to evaluate the company culture or determine how you might fit in with the team. It's a transaction that is purely based on your application materials. To handle this constructively, you should improve your cover letter and resume to meet the job requirements. Ask yourself if you need more experience, a higher profile in your field, or greater involvement in professional organizations.

Being invited to an interview can lead you to believe that you have a better chance of being hired. However, the emotional impact can be more severe if you are invited for an interview but are ultimately not selected for the job. The odds of being hired have significantly increased, and being rejected at this stage can be particularly difficult.

Despite your efforts to remain calm and collected, it's hard not to fantasize about job offers and envision a future with the company. This stage largely depends on how you present yourself and your performance, so it's difficult not to take a rejection personally and feel they didn't like you. If you're rejected after an interview, your initial reaction might be retaliating somehow, in shape, or form. You may feel like saying, "I didn't want your stupid job anyway!" But while it may provide temporary relief, negative words or actions can hurt you in the long run. Emotionally reacting after rejection can complicate an already tight job market, as you may have to interact with these people again in some other professional capacity. This is especially true if your field is small, and you might reencounter recruitment panel members in committee meetings or professional conferences. This could be awkward and embarrassing for you.

Offending a recruiter can also mean offending a potential network and may result in burning bridges you're unaware of. Networking is a crucial aspect of many jobs, and even though you may have been rejected for a particular position, you never know what the future holds. It's possible that the person who was hired may not stay in the role long-term, or the department may experience unexpected departures or extended leaves of absence, leading to a need for additional hiring. In such cases, recruiters may revisit previous candidates, and burning bridges may hinder your chances of being considered.

While it may be tempting to think that recruiters are out to get you, it's important to remember that they are people, too. They may have experienced similar rejections and may not enjoy rejecting candidates. Furthermore, conducting recruitment processes is time-consuming, and recruiters must balance their workloads with the recruitment process.

Your anger, bitterness, or insults won't harm the recruiter or change their mind and will only validate their decision to reject you. Despite the downsides of rejection, there are still potential benefits. It may lead to future job opportunities or expand your network. Therefore, approach the experience constructively by reflecting on areas for improvement. Take note of difficult questions and questions you could have asked, and assess how you presented yourself. Did you elaborate on your initial application effectively? Did you research the company beforehand? If you need to work on your interview skills, consider practicing. The interview process doesn't end with rejection; it's an opportunity to show your maturity, understanding of the profession, and worthiness as a candidate. Even if you weren't the first choice, how you handle the rejection can make a difference in future job searches. It's important to be ready for this possibility, as it could be the situation that leads to success.

Last but not least, send a thank you note for the opportunity they gave you to present your candidacy and mention that you are available for any new opportunity that might arise in their organization.

The Probation Period

"The only way to pass any test is to take it." - Unknown

In many jobs, especially when people hire remotely, there is a probation period. This is your time to be focused every day. Since you are now in the position, learn as much as you can about the organization, and ask as many questions as a six-year-old would do. Your enthusiasm, motivation, and capacity to integrate into the organization are even more critical. If you got hired because you have the required skills, the only question is, do you fit in the team? Are your teammates enjoying working with you and especially your superiors? Remember that it is not up to the team to make you feel welcome; it is your responsibility to integrate into the new team easily!

BEING INDISPENSABLE

"The key to making yourself indispensable is to consistently exceed expectations." - Unknown

Well, congratulation, you finally got the job. Now it is up to you to keep it. As I always said to my team: "The reason I hired you is that I know you can do the job. If you lose your job one day, it is because you fired yourself". Most people can't come to turn with that, but that is actually what happens in many cases.

Firing someone is a challenging decision. There are economic reasons which are behind the control of the manager. However, in most other cases, the employee triggers the consequences. Why would managers separate themselves from an asset in the team? Yes, you might lose your job because the company experience difficulties; even in those case, did you participate or share ideas that could have avoided the company's challenge? This is especially true in small organizations where each individual has a much more significant result to the bottom line.

In today's highly competitive job market, standing out from the crowd and making yourself indispensable to your employer is essential. To become essential in your job, you must demonstrate your value by consistently delivering high-quality results and a willingness to go above and beyond the call of duty. Here are some tips on how to become indispensable in your job.

Be proactive; one of the most important things you can do to become indispensable in your job is to be proactive. Don't wait for someone to tell you what to do. Instead, take the initiative and anticipate the needs of your employer. Identify potential problems and come up with solutions before they become significant issues. Take on additional responsibilities and make suggestions for how to improve processes or procedures. By being proactive, you show your employer that you are engaged, committed, and willing to take the lead.

Delivering high-quality results is another key to becoming indispensable in your job. Set ambitious goals for yourself and work hard to exceed them. Meet your deadlines and produce work that meets or exceeds your employer's expectations. Be willing to take on challenging tasks and demonstrate a can-do attitude. Focusing on results indicates that you are committed to achieving success and positively contributing to the organization.

To become indispensable in your job, be a problem solver. Problems will inevitably arise in any position, and the ability to solve them quickly and effectively is a valuable asset. Don't wait for someone else to come up with a solution. Instead, take the initiative and find a way to solve the problem. Use your creativity, resourcefulness, and critical thinking skills to develop innovative solutions that impress your employer. Being a problem solver demonstrates that you are proactive, solution-oriented, and committed to improving the organization.

Good communication skills are essential in any job; to become indispensable, you must communicate effectively with your colleagues, supervisors, and clients. Listen actively, ask questions, and ensure you understand your job's expectations and requirements. Speak clearly and concisely, and be willing to share your ideas and opinions. Use effective communication techniques, such as active listening, nonverbal cues, and empathy, to build strong relationships with those around you. Communicating effectively demonstrates that you are engaged, collaborative, and committed to achieving success.

No one succeeds on their own, and to become indispensable in your job, you need to be a team player. Work well with your colleagues and be willing to help others when needed. Collaborate effectively and contribute to a positive team dynamic. Be respectful, supportive, open-minded, and willing to compromise when necessary. By being a team player, you demonstrate that you are committed to achieving success for yourself and the organization as a whole.

To become indispensable in your job, you must be committed to continuous improvement. Be open to feedback and strive to improve your skills and knowledge. Attend training sessions, read industry news, and seek opportunities to learn new skills. Stay up-to-date with your field's latest trends and technologies, and be willing to experiment with new ideas and approaches. By continuously improving, you demonstrate that you are committed to personal and professional growth and ready to go the extra mile to succeed.

Consistently meet your commitments and deadlines. Your employer should be able to count on you to complete tasks and projects on time and to a high standard. This means being organized, managing time effectively, and prioritizing workload. By being reliable, you demonstrate your professionalism and your commitment to your job, and you earn the trust and respect of your employer and colleagues.

Finally, fostering positive relationships with colleagues, clients, and stakeholders is essential. Building relationships is a critical component of any successful career, and by doing so, you can position yourself as a valuable and influential team member. To build relationships effectively, you should be friendly, approachable, and supportive of others. This means actively listening to others, showing empathy and understanding, and being willing to lend a helping hand when needed. Building solid relationships can foster a positive and collaborative work environment, enhance communication and teamwork, and create career growth and development opportunities.

FINAL WORDS

'The best way to predict your future is to create it.' - Abraham Lincoln

As I completed the book's writing, one thought stood out to me; it is easy to get a job and even easier to keep it. However, the main problem for most people is that they need to learn how, and worse, they mostly have been taught the wrong thing regarding the entire job-hunting process. Too much emphasis is put on the trade itself and not enough on all the other aspects like communication and preparation. Most people would acknowledge that a passionate and self-motivated person is much more likely to be hired than a boring skilled person, but we still focus on the resume content. You cannot win a game if you don't know the rules. This book has been about teaching you the actual rules of the job-hunting game.

In my early twenties, I was applying for a developer position in Java. The only problem was that I didn't know Java. I did know other programming languages like C++; however, I was highly motivated to work with Java because it was the new upcoming language. I got an interview with one of the most prestigious Java companies at the time. The interview went well, but the interviewer told me I still needed to take the Java test. I reminded him that I didn't have any experience with Java. He told me: "Do your best." The result was a complete failure; I think I answered one or two questions and left all the others blank. Despite my total failure in the technical test, the manager told me in the last interview: "You're Hired!" and added: "I assume you are a fast learner." Fast learner? I don't remember we discussed that topic. So why did they hire me? Because they could not pass on a highly motivated, energetic, and well-spoken young man. And they were probably right; it took me only a few months to become one of the most skilled Java developers on the team. As I was a good team player, everyone was eager to teach me their best tricks.

Work on your competencies! With the advance of technology and the fact that more and more teams are decentralized, communication, for example, is an important skill; there are very few jobs in which you work alone. At least you need to deliver your work to a manager or a client. With proper communication skills, working with you would make it much more manageable. Time management is another critical skill to master. Adaptability, flexibility, problem-solving, and leadership are all skills that can be learned. You do not have to be born with those; it simply requires studying and applying yourself. It will give you an edge while performing your job and as a lifelong quality.

It always astonishes when people are excellent at their trade but are perceived as average because they lack essential competencies like knowing how to communicate efficiently or be organized in their work. On the other hand, someone with excellent competencies but just averaged at their trade might be considered an indispensable team member for all the add-on skills they provide.

Another focus of this book, and the dearest to my heart, has been to help people find a job they truly love. Yes, it is possible should you look for it rather than simply taking the first paycheck which comes your way. You want the word "work" to disappear from your vocabulary and be replaced with words like passion, dedication, and purpose. What better way to live your life?

Many people tell me: "I just need a job to get going, and then I can focus on finding my dream job." Let me ask you, did you just get married so you have a wife while you are looking for a better one? The problem with that train of thought is that it usually doesn't work out that way. People get stuck in their jobs for diverse reasons, and life moves on. Years later, their daughter asks them: "Dad, why are you so grumpy?". Maybe it has to do with the fact that you are doing a job you have to do rather than one you love doing. People underestimate the effect on their life of doing something they don't want to do. Are you struggling with your finance, or maybe in your marriage? Could it be related to spending eight hours of your day doing something you don't like? You might have settled for less than you deserve. Image doing that for forty years? On the other hand, how would your life turn out if, despite a long, challenging working day, you came home with a big smile, satisfied and contented with your daily accomplishments?

I hope you occasionally come back to the book as a reference and re-evaluate your situation, assess your competencies, and keep aligning your professional aspiration with your true self. Passion will make your job enjoyable, talents will make it easy, and competencies will make you the best at what you do. Truly knowing yourself and going after your dream job will give you such a tremendous edge that you will be acing all your interviews without a sweet. You might even turn the table around, and not only will they tell you: "You're Hired!" but possibly they will be insisting that you accept the job!

Printed in Great Britain
by Amazon

26979444R00116